# A Case for "GOOD WORDS"

*(To His Praise and Glory)*

**\*\*◊\*\***

## Barbara Griffith-Bourne

Sunesis Ministries Ltd

Copyright © 2019 Barbara Griffith-Bourne

The right of Barbara Griffith-Bourne to be identified as author of this work has been asserted by her in accordance with the Copyright, Designs, and Patents Act 1988

No part of this publication may be reproduced or transmitted in any form or by any means, electronic or mechanical, including photocopy, recording, or any information storage and retrieval system, without permission in writing from the author.

Scripture quotations are from the Holy Bible, New King James Version Copyright © 1982 Thomas Nelson, Inc. Used by permission.

Published by Sunesis Ministries Ltd. For more information about Sunesis Ministries Ltd, please visit:

www.stuartpattico.com

ISBN: 978-0-9956837-9-2

The views expressed in this book are solely those of the author and do not necessarily reflect the views of the publisher, and the publisher hereby disclaims any responsibility for them.

# Contents
◊***◊

| | |
|---|---|
| ◊ Why I was compelled to write this book | 7 |
| ◊ Aim of the book | 8 |
| ◊ About the Author | 11 |
| ◊ Acknowledgements | 13 |
| ◊ Dedication | 14 |
| ◊ Preamble | 15 |

## Chapter 1
**Qualifying 'the Case for Good Words'**    20
  : Questions we could ask ourselves    20
  : Poem – 'The Power of Thanksgiving'    34

## Chapter 2
**The authenticity of Good Words**    36
  : Poem – 'Awesome Creator'    37
  : The Source of good words    40

## Chapter 3
**Give the Young wholesome words**    42
  : Positive role models could help the young    49
  : Poem – 'The Sweet Sixteen Question'    51
  : Poem – 'Wilma –Foster Mother'    53
  : What Word-diet are we feeding the children?    54
  : Poem – 'A Purposeful Name'    59

## Chapter 4
**Leaders need Good Words**    61

: Poem – 'The Diamond Jubilee of Her Majesty the Queen'  61
: Poem – 'A Gracious Father'  63
: Poem – 'Father of Nations'  64

## Chapter 5
## Aspects of Good Words  67
: Pursue Good Words  75
: Poem – 'The Centurion's Faith'  78

## Chapter 6
## Good Words could work for you  80
: Poem – 'Salvation calls'  83

## Chapter 7
## A King's perspective on 'Good Words'  87

## Chapter 8
## Inappropriate Words could be wounding  93
: Scenarios  94
: Leaders' words should be honourable  96
: Mr Goodman versus Mr Negative  102
: Poem – 'Solomon'  104

## Chapter 9
## The consequences of Words  108

## Chapter 10
## Speak Good Words into your own life  114
: Poem – 'The fulfilled woman'  114
: Poem – 'The King's Daughter'  117
: Poem – 'Ophrah – an Icon'  118

  : Persist to speak 'Good Words' in dark moments    119

## **Chapter 11**
## **You could turn negativity around to good**    121
  : Adversity does not prevent good succeeding    121
  : Overcome negative encumbrance    123
  : Poem – 'Poetic deliverance'    124
  : People who succeeded in the face of adversity    126
  : Don't let jealous negativity hinder you – use your good talents    128
  : Poem – 'The Living Word'    131

## **Chapter 12**
## **Conclusion**    134
  : Profound lasting 'Good Words'    135
  : The A – Z Word    138
  : Poem – 'A rapturous moment'    139
  : Almighty God speaks to all people    140

## Why I was compelled to write this Book
**\*\*~\*\***

*Everyone loves compliments!*

*Most people are motivated by pleasantry; Good Words lift the Spirit; Good Words heal; Good Words change adverse situations; Good Words go where unpleasant words are not welcome; Good Words are life-changing; Good Words are beautiful!*

Some years ago, an alumni colleague, while reading one of my poems which I had written as a tribute for someone we both knew, exclaimed, "T*hese are good words! You don't often see words like these ...*"

Subsequently, while I was meditating on the 'Scriptures' on 20/01/13, I was prompted by 'Holy Spirit' for the second time to write a book entitled, **"A Case for Good Words";** therefore, I followed through with His help – To His Praise and Glory!

## _Aim of this Book_
!**!

My desire for the reader is that the **Poems** which are entwined in '**A case for good words**' would be inspiringly pleasurable, and '**the CASE**' itself compelling!

Poetry being my forte, I'm delighted to share with you yet another inspirational, 'Book of **'good words'** which, I believe will motivate and inspire you.

In my endeavour to bring a different twist to promote my beautiful poems, I've contended and built '**a case for good words'**. I am convinced that this concept would help people to:

* consider how important words are – especially **'good words'**
* endorse the sowing of **'good seeds'**
* support the young by displaying **good examples**
* promote an **environment of goodness**
* know that they could shake off negativity and become a POSITIVE thinker
* understand what our Heavenly Father **approves** and what He **reproves**

More importantly, **'the case'** explores the Biblical stance on goodness and God's perspective; that **good** should be established in the lives of individuals, thus benefiting the world in which we live.

Peace and Blessings to you!

**∗∗~∗∗**

**∗∗~∗∗**

In essence the Book is an exciting, thought provoking read. It serves also as a reference aid for meditation, reflection and pleasure.

The Author, Barbara Griffith-Bourne explores the uses and effect of **'good words'** against those of  and negative ones, providing necessary examples where appropriate. A quiz is included, should the reader desire to play a part.

This is Barbara Griffith-Bourne's 4th Book – poetry being the core and leading focus. Her first Book – "For His Glory" - the second, "For His Glory, Too", the third one – "Sucking Sugar

Cane – (Dreams in Paradise)", are all original inspirational Poems and have received great reviews. Copies are available for purchase from:

    Amazon

    The Publishers or

    The Author – E-mail: barbgriffbourne@hotmail.com

## *About the Author*

**~**

Born to parents from Barbados, Poet and Author, Barbara Griffith-Bourne was partly raised by her grandmother, a couture Seamstress and Evangelist who helped influence her passion for poetry by encouraging her and other family members to read portions from the Bible and classical literature, before bedtime.

Partly educated in Barbados, Barbara later immigrated to the United Kingdom to join her mother, where she continued and finished her education. When Barbara became a Christian, she prayed to receive the gift to write poetical lyric. This inspirational gift came as a result of a testing life's experience (she was unable to speak without stammering) which, at times for Barbara was very traumatic. Because God, the Father is faithful, she was delivered from this disorder during her early twenties.

Barbara's **desire now has been truly realised for His purpose** - to be of great inspirational help to others through her written and **spoken words**!

Although she enjoys writing poetry, her focus is on the **'spoken word'** for which she has, for many years undertaken **'Poetic Recitals'** at various events nationally and internationally, which brought much inspiration, pleasure and refreshment to people in diverse audiences. She has been privileged to use her poetic gift to bless listeners on mediums such as BBC Radio Berkshire, Voice of Barbados, Faith World TV and several other media-engaged audiences - to the Glory of God, the Father!

**~**

# Acknowledgements

*~*

I give special thanks to the late Elbertha Griffith and the late Reverend McDonald Griffith, my parents, who dedicated my life to the glory of God and taught me to love the Lord and were very instrumental in focussing my mind heavenward. Peace to them.

Special thanks to the late Elizabeth Small, my grand-mother, who influenced my childhood years with Christian principles. (The poem, 'A Virtuous Woman', in Book 1 and 2) is dedicated to her memory. Peace is hers!

Special thanks also and appreciation to Lukas, my grand-son, for his input and assistance with this work and technical help; most of all for his **interest and encouragement** in propelling the 'For His Glory Vision'. May the Grace and Favour of the Lord rest upon him always!

There are **numerous other names** in my immediate family, friends and relatives as well as the **'Church family'** which I could add to this list who have **spoken good words over my life**, **who have prayed for me** and who have been sources of **great support** and **encouragement** – *you know who you are! M*ay your reward from our Heavenly Father be very great.

Giving credit to who credit is due; I feel compelled to give exceptional thanks to my cousin, Tanya Alleyne who willingly loan me her laptop so I could get started on the manuscript for this book when I was in Barbados during a period in 2013.

# *Dedication*

**\*\*~\*\***

I lovingly dedicate this book to **'THE CREATOR OF GOOD WORDS'** - THE KING OF KINGS AND THE LORD OF LORDS – Almighty God!

I express my heartfelt gratitude for His consistent inspiration, wisdom, knowledge, understanding and help, without which the writing of this book would not be possible – in Him I live, move and have my being – I love you, Father God!

**\*\*~\*\***

# To His Praise and Glory

## (A case for "GOOD WORDS")

### PREAMBLE

***Pleasant words*** are like a honeycomb, **sweetness** to the soul and **health** to the bones. (Proverbs 16v24).

Anxiety in the heart of man causes depression, but **a *good word* makes it glad.** (Proverbs 12v25).

A man has **joy** by the answer of his mouth, and a **word spoken** in **due season**, how ***good it is!*** (Proverbs 15v23).

It is universally accepted that **'GOOD WORDS'** are <u>preferable</u> to bad, ugly or inappropriate words. Good Words are powerful! Bad words too are powerful, but they carry a damaging and adverse effect. In our world today where negative words are on the increase alongside a flow of futile profanity, there is **a need for 'Good Words'** to combat the trend of profane and negative speaking, thus lifting high the banner of godliness! Principally, **Good Words** are like:

**  A Healing balm to the Emotion;

**  Sweet Music to the Ears, and;

**  Comfort to the Soul!

(In stating my case, my view is from both the temporal and spiritual aspect of life).

All humans with the power of speech have a choice to speak good or ill with their tongue. It is a true saying and, even a fact that, a person could **change destinies by the words that they speak!**

## FOOD FOR THOUGHT!

*"I create the fruit of the lips: Peace, peace to him who is far off and to him who is near", says the LORD, and I will heal him."* (Isaiah 57v19).

*A man's stomach shall be satisfied from the fruit of his mouth; from the produce of his lips he shall be filled.* (Proverbs 18v20).

***You are snared by the words of your mouth; you are taken by the words of your mouth;*** ... (Proverbs 6v2).

**!!! Everyone produces fruits from their lips every time they speak, whether good or bad! What type of fruits will drop from your lips today?**

One day as I was resting my head on the Bible in place of my pillow and thinking of the profound usefulness of the 'Word of God', this poem burst forth in my spirit:

## My Uses of 'The Word'

On God's Word I rest as my **pillow**
For peaceful comfort in stormy weather;
- (Jacob used a rugged stone
When in the wilderness alone);
He clung to an Angel for a blessed word;
'Prince of God' was the word he heard!

I use **'the Word'** in uncertain doubt
To work difficult **puzzles** out;

I use **'the Word'** as acceptable speech
Giving instruction my tongue to **teach**!
I use **'the Word'** as my **hobby**;
It's a **pleasure** and inspiration to me;
Its topics are so profoundly diverse -
I draw **sweetness** when it I rehearse!

**'The Word'** is my **beauty** regime
Expelling prideful and evil schemes
So beautiful humility is seen!
It's my daily **cleansing** routine,
In its washing I'm made pristine!

**'The Word'** is my sure **spotlight**
Leading the way in the darkest night!
**'The Word'** I lovingly retain
As the Holy Spirit makes it plain;
He wisely it elucidates
In my heart to saturate!
**'The Word'** is my effective **prayer-tool**,
Great results I gain from Wisdom's school!

**'The Word'** is my spiritual **food** –
Bread of Life - whatever my mood!
My Living Water, my **refreshment**
That I drink to my heart's content!
God's **Word** – my spiritual **eyes** to see,
My understanding enlightening free!
**'The Word'** is my **time-check**
So Jesus' return I won't forget!

❖✧❖

The true **Word** profoundly spoken
Breaks doubt plainly **open**;–
Why should the Logos be a mystery?
Smothered or hidden be?
'The Word' is my capable **Teacher**,
My **health** and Divine **Healer**!
In my weakness, God's **strength**
Is perfected at great length!

❖✧❖

'The Word' is my **Mentor** and **Guide**
In its footsteps, I cannot slide!
It is also my **Defence** –
A two-edged sword in every sense!
'The Word' is my **sure Refuge**,
The ultimate safety, I've often proved!
It is my daily **medicine**,
My **antidote** and virus prevention!
'The Word' is my spiritual **covering** –
Garment of praise, **anxiety defeating**!
'The Word' is my faithful Virtue,
Moulding my characteristics too!
'The Word' is my **complete** satisfaction;
In all, my **cup** of salvation!
The Living Word - Jesus Christ
Is my sure Eternal Life!

❖✧❖

(In stating my case, my view is both from the temporal and spiritual aspect of life).

# CHAPTER 1

## QUALIFYING THE GOOD WORD CASE

In qualifying this 'case for good words', we might have many questions to ask ourselves; among which are the following:

- Is Light preferred to Darkness?

- Is Darkness preferred to Light?

- Who welcomes good words?

- Is there a time for good words?

- Could there be a hindrance to good words being conveyed?

Again, we may want to consider how words are communicated – via Pictures; Speaking (publicly or privately); Writing Letters, Fax; E-mail; Reading; Music; Television; Songs; Telephone; Books; Internet; Mobile-phone and other various medium.

## Further questions we could ask ourselves:

- What affect do words have on me?

- How do I receive words?

- Do I re-act to words, good or bad?

- How do words make me feel?

- Do they make me feel empty?

- Do they make me feel angry?

- Do they uplift me?

- Do they zap my confidence or uplift me?

- Do they empower me?

- Do they make me feel vulnerable?

- Do they affect my thought pattern?

This list of questions could go on and on but, <u>the fact of the matter is that words, good or bad could affect us in some form or fashion during our life time</u>.

## Some Types and Quality of Words

We would agree that words could be **GRAPHICAL**, **WRITTEN**, **SPOKEN** and/or **SENT** whether for **positive** or <u>negative</u> means. Again, we could accept that words are more often than not motivated by a person's mood, circumstances or by pre-meditation.

Again, it is true that, whether words are written, spoken, graphical or expressed by any other **good means**, they could covey comfort, healing, empowerment, inspiration and hope. Also true, is the fact that ill, bad or an inappropriate word could be destructive.

## GRAPHICAL WORDS

A myriad of people around the globe view adverse graphical words every day in some form or another without realising the weight that some of these graphical words carry and what affect they could have on the lives of those who view them. Among these are Bill boards and other ill forms of advertisements enticing one and all to buy their wares.

Some Billboards carry offensive pictures of near nude bodies or two persons in suggestive and uncompromising acts. When displayed in the public domain, I believe these send out harmful and negative messages, especially to young children.

## WRITTEN WORDS

Without naming any, I deem true that there are numerous <u>positive</u> good inspirational books written that target the human mind, body and spirit to uplift and encourage. However, among the good books that I've read, I would recommend the World's best seller - <u>the 'Bible</u> Scripture' which is the complete manual for all aspect of life's existence and which <u>contains wholesome words</u> for all. We can connect with the teachings of the 'Bible Scripture' through nature, history and the behaviour of humans and other living creatures.

To the contrary, there are various books and written statements which distort the truth about the Good Words of the 'Scriptures'; for example - the origin of humans. Some claim that humans derive from the Ape and Monkey family; yet they cannot tell or convincingly explain why humans are being born without tails! (This type of written information only produces negative thinking and I doubt it would inspire anyone; it might only send them on a futile quest.).

## SPOKEN WORDS

Whether we care to believe it or not, the truth of the matter is that the **Spoken Word** is from the beginning of time, the first **GOOD WORDS** were spoken by Almighty God, the Creator, whose good words brought the Universe into being. The powerful, positive, good and awesome words, spoken by the Creator of the universe caused light to overcome the darkness – Then God said, "Let there be light"; and there was light. (Genesis 1v3) – proving that **a good word is a light**. **He** further commended all his work and saw that it was **'very good'**. (see Genesis 1v31).

To the contrary, some in the fallen world might not agree with the above, as they claim that the universe came about as a result of a 'Big Bang' – ascertaining that it came about without the existence of Almighty God's input; denying His existence!

So far, I have not heard that anyone has ever met the acquaintance of 'Mr Big Bang'; (how irresponsible of Mr Big Bang to disappear without wanting to form a relationship with humans? (Smile)!

Again, I do not see Mr 'Big Bang' every time the rain

falls or when the Farmers' crops bring forth fruit from the seeds planted?

More dominantly, Almighty God - the Creator, says in his Holy Scriptures, *"For as the rain comes from heaven and returns not there, but waters the earth and makes it bring forth and bud, that it may give seed to the sower and bread to the eater; so shall My word be that goes forth out of My mouth, it shall not return unto Me void, but it shall accomplish that which I please and it shall prosper in the thing whereto I sent it"*, (Isaiah 55v10-11).

(As we live, we see proof of these **good words** that Almighty God has spoken e.g.; in <u>all aspects of nature</u>).

## WISDOM
**~**

**Wisdom cries out to all,
Unto the Young' and Old It calls;
It's calling now at your gate –
'Come, embrace it for goodness sake'!
In life's path it gives understanding
That leads to <u>life's</u> refreshing Fountain!**

## CONSIDER THIS!!

If you were to enter a darkened room, or be in a forest at night and you decide to turn on the appropriate light, or if you initiate some type of light - matches, a torch or lantern - to the darkened area, there would be a <u>profound effect</u>.

According to Genesis chapter 1, **the whole universe was in darkness – God said, "let there be light" … – SPEAKING to the Sun, Moon and Stars to enter the overwhelming darkness that existed then; when the <u>light entered the darkness of the universe</u>**, I believe, as expected, **there would've been, a profound effect! After all, the universe is phenomenally vast!** Moreover, what we see of the universe lines up with the <u>'biblical scripture' account</u> in Genesis chapter 1.

Moreover, we've all heard the loud and frightening bang of the 'THUNDER and LIGHTNING'?

My conclusion – **NO 'BIG BANG' affect WITHOUT**

**ALMIGHTY GOD!**

(After all, if there is no God, there would be no need for people to choose right over wrong! More importantly, God was the one who implemented the right judgement and true laws – highlighting that we should love our neighbour as ourselves.

Some say they can't see God, so they don't think He exists. We cannot see Him with our natural eye but He still exists; (has anyone ever seen a tooth ache or a headache?). The Bible Scripture documents that God is Spirit – (Jesus' words written in St John 4 v 24). We would accept that we humans are **Spirit**, **Soul** and **Body** – our body is seen but our Spirit and Soul is not seen - ?true. Why then should it be so strange that we cannot see Almighty God because He is Spirit? He tells us that our sins (evil doings) have separated us from Him. (Isaiah 59v2).

**We would agree that we have all done evil acts at some time or another)!**

## **TIME**
\*\*_\*\*

Time... precious time -
Its usefulness is for us to find!
'Time' is life's profound commodity,
Bearing treasures of opportunity!
Time ... to seek our purpose
In life's chaotic circus!
Time and chance happens to all -
How do you respond to its call?
\*\*_\*\*

**A word fitly spoken is like apples of gold in settings of silver.** (Proverbs 25v11).

If ever I had thought that I was a "one-person band" <u>who promotes **good words**</u> and positive thinking, I would have been mistaken! On 24/02/14 whilst travelling on a bus to town, a little girl (about five years old) boarded the bus I was travelling on with her mother and baby sister; they came near where I was sitting and the little girl started to wave good-bye to a young school boy at the bus stop whom they were previously in conversation with. The mother turned to the little girl and said something to her; immediately, I heard the little girl shouted this to her mother: "STOP SAYING HE'S A LOSER, HE'S A WINNER"! I was certainly amazed at the little girl's response to her mother's comments and was very much encouraged that there are others, like myself, promoting positive good words; as the saying goes – 'a little child shall lead them'!

The story goes that, a couple's marriage relationship suffered a rocky patch when, the wife with negative sharp words, accused the husband of not loving or caring for her on account that, she thought he had forgotten their wedding anniversary. It was the end of the day and as he did not produce a present straight away on entering their home from work; "You do not love me", the wife exclaimed - not realising that her husband had hidden the present and was waiting to give it to her at dinner; in the heated moment, the husband retaliated by exclaiming, 'you don't deserve the present I bought you, you just couldn't wait, could you'?... (This shows how negative words could easily destroy a relationship).

Job uttered these words to his friends: *"**How long will you torment my soul, and break me in pieces with words**"?* These friends had come to comfort him after they had heard about the death of his children and cattle. (See Job 19v2). In reading the biblical account of Job, it would appear that his friends were apportioning blame to him for his grief, rather than being just good listeners!

## SENT WORDS

The <u>sent word</u> came into play when, the children of Israel were in dire straits and there was no one to help them; they then cried out to the Lord. Scripture tells us that - **He sent His word and healed them and delivered them from their destructions**. (Psalms 107v20). We read that this **good word** which was **sent** produced <u>positive results</u>.

The example of the Centurion in the Bible story is one to be reckoned with. He believed that <u>good words could be sent</u> that would bring forth positive results. He asked Jesus to speak/send the healing word to his sick servant who was at home, rather than go to his house; this proved true when Jesus obliged him and the servant was healed. (See St Luke 7v 1-10).

Once, enquiring about the welfare of a friend's children, my friend told me that they were living some distance away, but that she usually **sends words of blessing and protection to them in prayerful declarations**. (We could agree that in prayer <u>good words could be sent</u> that become effective - Words <u>sent</u> in Faith has no distance for effectiveness!

More significantly, this is why Jesus in his teachings says that people should always pray and not lose heart. (See St Luke 18v1).

These examples and similar ones show that words could be sent verbally to others even though they are not physically present. Jesus taught his disciples to pray – (sending petitions/thanksgiving) to 'Our Father (God) who is in heaven'; (See St Matthew 6v9-13).

While growing up, I've experienced where <u>negative verbal words</u> sent from one person in my neighbourhood to another via a child, produced ugly results. The adult woman in question sent contentious words via the child of another woman whom she had fallen out with. The words were delivered and resulted in a physical fight between the two families which brought much tension throughout in our neighbourhood.

Notably, from a biblical stance, Almighty God who **sets the trend of life in His Word, highlights things that he hates or cannot tolerate;** Proverbs chapter 6, verses 16-19 tells us:

*"These six things the LORD hate: yes, seven are an abomination to him:*

*A proud look;*

*A lying tongue,*

*Hands that shed innocent blood,*

*A heart that devises wicked plans,*

*Feet that are swift in running to evil;*

*A false witness who speaks lies*

*And one who sows discord among brethren.*

(As we can see, all of the above in some way are inherent in evil; whether expressed or devised in the heart).

✧❖✧

**!!! "A good word costs no more than a bad one"** - (An English Proverb)!

✧❖✧

**!!! "Don't speak unless you can improve on the silence"** - (A Spanish Proverb)!

**~**

If you like playing with words, here is a quick quiz! - Put the phrases below in a fitting category) - **FALSE:** ‡

**TRUE:** ☆    **DISAGREE:** §    **REASON:** §‡☆

Words harm!

Words sow seeds!

Words heal!

Words shape destinies!

Words Kill!

Words make alive!

Words brighten a path!

Words kindle a fire!

Words darken a path!

Words give counsel!

Words bring Favour!

Words quench anger!

Words bring guidance!

Words destroy Kingdoms!

Words don't count!

Words don't mean anything!

*Expressing gratitude should be a vocal act;*
*Using one's voice as a matter of fact;*
*Good words make all the difference,*
*Notably, as a point of reference!*

*Giving thanks to God and his praises sing*
*Is always a very good thing*
*Declared Israel's powerful King!*

## "THE POWER OF THANKSGIVING"

*+*+*+*

The attitude which God highly ranks
Is the one to always give Him thanks!
It's the mark of innate humility;
Trusting Him for soulful possibility!
Praise Him from whom all providence flow;
In sincerity – let it show!
True gratitude sweet blessings will attract
When your heart sends thanksgiving back;
This powerful engaging effect
In earnest the 'Truth' respects!
In all things we're admonish to be grateful
Whether we're empty or full!
If the Apple-tree its fruits do not bare;
On the Corn-stalk no shoots appear;
When the Cattle have no grass to eat,
Nor the Grape-vine has no meat,
Give thanks before your blessing you receive -
Enacting Faith's power to conceive!
Count your blessings and give thanks,
Trusting not in riches or the high street Banks;

God will restore what the enemy has stolen;
He will make good what Satan has broken –
Raining down upon you sweet Favour
For each and every endeavour;
He will turn back the drought for sure;
Giving you abundantly more!
It's amazing what 'Thanksgiving' can do
When you count past blessings anew –
It takes the sting out of worry;
Uplifting your Spirit in a hurry;
Opening the doors to blissful Joy
And a new song on your lips employ;
That's the power of 'Thanksgiving'
The sweetness from God, the Father's Blessing!

## CHAPTER 2

## **THE AUTHENTICITY OF 'GOOD WORDS'**

The authenticity of 'the Word of Almighty God' - the Holy Bible Scriptures, **is the leading force for Good Words and is the foundation of it all.** In these Good Words are sound <u>instructions</u> and <u>guidance</u> for every condition of life. Good words should not be thrown away but cherished ... written upon the tables of your heart to inspire another. Bible Scripture is the basis for **Good Words** and could be applied to all aspects of life's situations with profound results, should an individual adhere to it.

King David gave credence to this fact, in that he said, **"The entrance of your words give light; it gives understanding to the simple".** (Psalms 119 v 130).

People say, "Sticks and stones will break my bones but words won't hurt"... - but, it is a fact that bodily wounds may heal quicker than an emotional scar when inappropriate or evil words are said to someone).

Perhaps, this is why Brother James place emphasis on the **'taming of the tongue'** (See St. James, chapter 3).

***And the LORD answered the angel who talked to me, with good and comforting words.*** *(Zechariah 1v13).*

***By the word of the LORD the Heavens were made, and all the host of them by the breath of His mouth.*** *(Psalms 33v6).*

A Poem to the Praise and Honour of the Creator, '**the Author of GOOD WORDS'**, who gave me these beautiful words to convey:

## Awesome Creator

Awesomely, Beautiful You!
All Glory rightly assigned is your due!
The Beauty of your **Love** is ever new,
Immeasurable, not hidden from view!
Lighting up the world like a beacon of gold
Ensuing powerfully at Creation bold!
Your 'trademark' that describes you best
Is your innate Beauty of Holiness!
Your **awesome presence** is an experience
Of blissful alluring ambience!

❖◊❖

**Purpose** is entrench in your creativity,
Springs of Love – your Awesome Beauty!
The glorious burst of daily **sunrise** –
Exuberant health from God, **so wise**!
The **flower-fields** adorn so picturesque,
**Buds** bursting forth in glorious zest!
**Rugged hills** and mountainous **landscape**;
Magnificently shaped **clouds** so ornate
Depicting moving theatrical arts,
Each pattern formed playing their parts!
Marvellous **trees** and **plant** life;
**Marine organisms** countless, rife!
The splendid scenic **sunset**,
Once seen, not easy to forget!
❖◊❖
The misty **fog,** a greyish mask;
The **dazzling dew** coating the **green grass**!
The boisterous claps of **thunder**,
That makes **human hearts** shudder!
The terror of the flashing **lightning**;
The **stormy rain** of providential **blessing**!
Invisible **winds** destroying high towers,
Demonstrates your mighty powers!
The exquisite treasures of **snowflakes**;
Frost resembling crumbles of frozen cakes!
The tranquil **waters** of the flowing **stream**,
Meandering through the **valley** like a dream!
The spectacular gushing **waterfall**
Resplendent as a whitened wall!
❖◊❖
The roar of the **Lion**, the purr of the **cat**

Convey your vociferous act!
Tiny **creatures** living under the **earth**,
Slowly emerging, showing their worth!
**Birds** singing out your beauty loud,
Joyfully soaring under the **cloud**!
**Oceanic waters** of the boisterous **waves**,
Proudly crashing upon **rocks** and **caves**!
The force of the swirling **Tornadoes**;
Explosive eruption of **volcanoes**;
Destructive action of **Earthquakes**;
Causing fearful cries of mercy make!
The **starry sky**, a luminous masterpiece,
Strikingly bright for the **eyes** to feast!
Your beauty enshrines the **universe**,
Yet, you focus on **people** first!
Everything you created **is real**,
They spell out your **Love** in great detail;
However we tour the **creation** circle,
Your designs are breathtakingly beautiful!

❖◊❖

The beauty of your **Law** is easy to decipher –
It says, 'as you love yourself, love one another'!
You poured your **Love in the human** heart;
In Redemption you left your indelible mark
So we could on your word rely
And with you, the Creator complies;
Allowing Jesus to give his **life** for us at Calvary,
Expresses **your most** awesome **Beauty** -
Giving all people a chance to be
With you and **rest** throughout eternity!
You added 'the **key**' of Faith's decree

Aiding us to **trust** you ultimately!
Father, 'give us grace' is our plea,
Always to **worship** your exalted dignity!

## The Source of 'Good Words'

The existence of the Universe gives credence to the true claim that it was brought into being by the 'SOURCE of GOOD WORDS' by Almighty God, the Creator. ***In the beginning was the Word and the Word was with God, and the Word was God. He was in the beginning with God. All things were made through Him, and without Him nothing was made that was made.*** (St John 1v1-3).

Time began with the Good Word by the Creator and time will end also with His Good Words - revealed to and given to St. John the Apostle by Jesus Christ: ***The Angel whom I saw standing on the sea and on the land raised up his hand to heaven and swore by Him that lives forever and ever, who created Heaven and the things that are in it, the earth and the things that are in it and the sea and the things that are in***

*it, that there should be delay no longer ...).*
*(Revelation 10 v5-6).*

In our world today many who are in the limelight and media look to big-up their name, yet some of them do not have anything of substance to say. But Almighty God knew how effective **'good words'** could be that He puts his own perspective to His Word; ...For You have magnified Your word above all Your name. (See Psalms 138v2).

# CHAPTER 3

## GIVE THE YOUNG WHOLESOME WORDS

We are in 'a climate of great concern for young people's bad behaviour' and their lack of enthusiasm and motivation to become meaningful individuals. While some people blame culture, upbringing, poverty or lack of activities and resources, others place the blame on lack of good role models and absent fathers who should be playing a part in their children's lives.

Nevertheless, I believe that **young people benefit greatly from affirmation**. Where there are Uncles, Aunts, Grandmothers and other relatives available, they could still make an impact on a young life by **passing on a good word** of encouragement here and there to them, should they listen or not. Good words from School Teachers could also help shape a young person's future success. (May the God of Heaven and earth Bless those relatives, parents, Foster parents and caring organisations that are, and have been doing their part to help and encourage the young).

Just as senior folk needed affirmation when they were young, the youths of today need good words, more so. (I

<u>remember that I needed it</u>).

Some of these old sayings have been used over and over and have proven to encourage many:

- "you may not have a job yet, but you have great potential"...

- "don't give up, keep on trying; you will make it"...

- "you may not pass first time, but a second or a third try means

   you'll be even better at it"...

- "behind every dark cloud, there is a silver lining"...I'd tell my son this!)

- "where there's life, there is hope"...

- "your best is the best that you can do"...

- "where there's a will, there's a way"...

- "you've got great talents, don't hide your light under a bushel"...

- "Rome was not built in a day, so you'll achieve your goals, given time"...

- "well done"!

-"you are looking bright today, son; take care"...

- "you did that job well, I'm pleased with you"...

- "if at first you don't succeed, try, try and try again – you'll get

there ...

"look on the bright side, it is always the better side"...

- "joy is being at peace with yourself and your maker, don't stress

unnecessarily"...

- "it's good to have a heart of gratitude"...

- "manners (respect) make the man"...

- "patience is a good virtue"...

- "do good and good will follow you"...

A person I knew who would always found time for young

people was my grandmother; especially when she travelled the length and breadth of the Island, Barbados as an Evangelist. She would always speak **good encouraging words** to the young in her travels (whether an individual or a group), especially, should she see any of them up to mischief or playing pranks; (they respected her for that). She has left a lasting legacy of good admonition so much so that some people **who were young in that era still talk about her good**. Equally, she much encouraged her offspring and others in her district with wholesome words in that, she was one of the first ports of call for help - she was locally known as "Mammy".

Many may argue that, speaking to or correcting young people poses a security risk. However, I maintain still that a good word spoken to a young person never go amiss and would always be fruitful although, they may not regard or appreciate it at the time. (I must confess that my heart for young people allows me to overcome fear of reprisal to engage and speak a good word to them; sometimes I'm laughed at by some of them, but others would thank me or say to their friends, "she's right you know", as they would listen).

**In the circumstances, I am not giving a licence to anyone to put themselves in the firing line for attack, should they see any threatening behaviour from a young person; they would have to follow their heart.**

Mistakes in the past have been made by parents, teachers and guardians when they may, in anger, pronounced ill words, like the ones below, upon children and young people in their care. However, I deem these humiliating: I've heard both teachers, parents and other adults use these demeaning words to children; (I could confess that I've been called some, if not all of these): -

- Stupid
- Loser
- Empty head
- You 'good for nothing'
- You dyslexic person
- Jack ass

* Ugly
* Idiot
* Pea brain
* You numb skull
* You're a failure

Thinking about the impact of these ill words, it's like feeding 'bad food' to someone's emotion. We all need <u>to practice</u> using more **uplifting words** of affirmation to the youth, **should we desire the best for them.**

There are occasions when children are belittled when adults wrongly categorise children academically, assuming and affirming that a child has average ability. This I've heard from a child – "my teacher said that I'm only a 'C' student"; yet this child had the ability to excel beyond a 'C', and she did! This motto could be adopted by all students:

"LET YOUR GOOD BE BETTER AND YOUR BETTER BECOMES YOUR BEST"!

Believe it or not, thousands of people are still enslaved emotionally due to negative words spoken over their lives while growing up!

I recently watched a documentary on television and was saddened by the tears of a middle aged woman who was still held captive by the ill words spoken by her father to her that continue to affect how she sees herself and her attitude to life itself. She said her father told her while she was growing up that she was stupid. He would make her repeat it again and again. Sadly, despite professional counselling help, this lady found it difficult to move on and confessed that she thinks she is stupid still.

There is a demise of good morals and good values in this generation and never had there been so many prison establishments in any era. Perhaps some fault for children's **bad behaviour** stems from the falling off of **good practice that breeds good morals and good values,** leaving people questioning why crime is so rampant.

Attending school in Barbados and in the UK, both of my schools had pupil assembly in the mornings before class when, we acknowledged thanksgiving in songs and prayers to God, the Creator. The Head-teacher would also update the assembly on any one who was sick or in hospital and would pray for that person – showing that we should care for each other. Sometimes the class assembly had to repeat the 10 Commandments which were the fundamental principles that taught good living. (Somehow, it appears that of late, the ruling educational bodies, for whatever reason, do not often or not at all include this good practice in the schools' agenda).

More significantly, young people could be <u>encouraged</u> in the fact that, **whatever their ability, they could make a difference for good to their world in some way** since there are numerous paraplegics, sight and speech impaired people who have and are impacting their world in Sports, the Arts, motivational speaking and even caring for others.

## POSITIVE ROLE MODELS COULD HELP THE YOUNG

Young people need more good role models for them to emulate! Our world could greatly benefit from an abundance of **positive good words**; especially being spoken over the lives of young people! Parents, guardians and those who minister to them in the home, kindergarten, schools, colleges, university and other institutions have the privilege to make a great and lasting impact on young people.

What is said to a young person or **how they make them feel** could act as a **'lifetime gift'** or a 'destructive blow' to their emotions'. (Forgive me for saying this - but somehow, it would appear that some of us adults do not have much tolerance or compassion for the young. Some seem to forget that they too were young once when, they themselves did some of the same things as young people and have behaved in some of the same ways).

I know there are many others in our world who are pushing 'the chariot of positivity' forward – holding motivational seminars and events of 'positivity thinking' and such like, although it all seems like a drop in the ocean against 'the massive 'cloud of negativity' that surrounds us at times. Albeit, I believe it is necessary for me to add my contribution as a stepping stone of goodness.

The Young look up to people in the public eye, especially in the media, the music and film industry; this could be a good opportunity for these icons to send out the right vibes to the young. However, I am disappointed that some lyrics do nothing to uplift young people! They could much more be motivated if more influential people, who have a myriad following, send out **encouraging strong positive messages** to them, letting them know that they have value; they have potential and there is a purpose for which to live, causing them to think about their life's worth. Equally, they will especially benefit from the wisdom of God's Words which will guide them along the right paths of life.

This poem was especially written with young people in mind – (some are anxious to reach age 16):

## The Sweet Sixteen Questions
~**~

Does 'sweet sixteen' means
That you've awaken from childhood's dream
Controlled by parental discipline
Where your life was all hemmed in?
Does it mean you can stay out very late?
And all chastisement forsake?
~**~

Have you escaped parental responsibility
Because you've experienced mere puberty?
Does it mean you'll shed no more tears?
Having left behind your primary years?
Would you no longer have to be told?
Or even be scold?
~**~

Would you not heed instructions?
Given to you for Godly directions?
Do you now know everything?
Thinking you have turned an adult at 16?
Should you not embrace 'wisdom's reproof?
At this remarkable stage of your youth?
~**~

Wisdom is more precious than gold
And is relevant for both young and old;
The start of wisdom is to reverence the Lord,
Embracing his truth in accord!
Let wisdom be your special delight,
It will guide and teach you right!
~**~

Much encouragement and prayers are needful now more than ever as we constantly hear of young people being drawn away into gangs and other evil persuasions; yet, these good words from Bible Scripture give warning and persuade them not to join in evil acts:

*My son, if sinners entice you, do not consent. If they say, "Come with us, let us lie in wait to shed blood; let us lurk secretly for the innocent without cause;...... my son, do not walk in the way with them, keep your foot from their path; for their feet run to evil, and they make haste to shed blood.* (Proverbs 1 v 10-16).

Wilma, a Foster Mother who cared for hurting children and young people over decades spoke much good into their lives and encouraging them that they have purpose and value. This poem is a tribute to her memory:

*... Because she cared —*
*... Helping others, her life she shared!*
~*~
Wilma, we ascribe to you a "Tribute" -

In celebrating your life, we salute!
Recognising your "Gift of Love and Compassion",
We extend to you our hearty appreciation!
You were given to us for only a season -
Having fulfilled your purpose you left a shining Beacon!
When there were not many to care
You Wilma compassionately were there!
A call to the nation went out;
More like a resounding shout -
"Children, children, hurting children;
Who will have compassion on them"?
You answered, "Some I will rescue –
Helping one or a few...
To them I'll open my door,
I'll show compassion, more and more"!
For them you dedicated your life
Easing their turmoil and emotional strife;
Combining them with your own family
You'd bring them to spend time together by the sea
In keeping the bond of family unity!
In this you were immensely supportive,
Precious time and resources you'd kindly give;
A "Gold Medal" is meant for you
And joyous accolades too;
You left a legacy that is great,
Good qualities for others to emulate!
You acted as Nurse, Confidante and Carer
Standing strong as Home-maker and Mother;
Up late at nights and sometimes before dawn,
Caring and consoling in the bleak morn;
Preparing meals, taking the children to school

Portraying skilful acts, defying ridicule!
You juggle other commitments with homecare
Bringing multi-tasking into play;
You did it in kindness and confidence,
Demonstrating Love with Excellence!
You were a Mum, Grand-Nan and Grandmother;
A Sister, Auntie, Cousin, Friend and Daughter;
You're well-loved and respected -
Your good qualities are there to be coveted!
You've made a 'grand contribution' to your world –
One more precious than a pearl!
The loss of your presence we'll sadly regret,
Your welcoming smile we won't forget;
However, your memory will live on in our heart
Until we meet again, when we'll never part!

**(Dedicated to the memory of Wilma Ogden)**

~*~

## What 'Word-diet' are we feeding the Children?

We hail and celebrate all others who help encourage the young at the most vulnerable stage of their lives!

More significantly, the Lord God gives hope as in ***Jeremiah chapter 29 verses 11: For I know the thoughts that I think towards you, says the Lord, thoughts of peace and not of evil, to give you a*** *future and a hope.*

In every generation there is some great man or woman who has changed the course of history and their world for the better where **the root of their success were good words spoken to them when they were young.** <u>The same could be true for some others who hurt their world because of ill words that were spoken to them in some way</u>; although, we've seen some who had the good spoken to them and did not make good use of it! Yet, some others who had suffered negatively turned it around **positively**).

Parents have a responsibility to rear their offspring in line with the will of Almighty God, instilling **good morals** and **good values** in them at an early stage in their lives, even from the womb, in order to shape their destiny. I know of some parents who have read books to their baby or had exposed them frequently to music whilst still in the womb; (just as babies love the taste of milk, they would develop and desire a taste for whatever they are exposed to, good or bad, as they grow).

Perhaps, this is why the Apostle Peter in his writings urged the new believers in Christ to reject malice and all evil speaking; He says: ... *as new born babes, desire the pure milk of 'the word' (of God); that you may grow thereby* ... (1Peter 2v2).

Children need good morals and good values taught and shown to them for them to grow in wisdom and good understanding about life and its challenges and how to cope when adversity presents itself to them.

It is sad to see children being rude to parents in public and displaying temper tantrums, although some of their behaviour does not necessarily reflect how the parents rear/teach them. We sometimes dress our children in attire bearing negative words like - REBEL; ANGRY DUDE; RUDE BOY; CHEEKY MONKEY; LITTLE MONSTER, etc. etc.- although some of these labels may tickle our senses and make us smile, it could be difficult in later years to erase some labels! I remember when I was growing up nearly everyone had a nickname which was not very appealing and which they became ashamed of when they grew up. They refuse to accept these nick names or respect anyone who would address them by these names.

*A good name is to be chosen rather than great*

***riches*** ... (Proverbs 22v1).

I believe somehow that words have vibes/a spirit attached to them, whether good or bad. If these words – good or bad are embraced / practiced long enough, the spirit of the word attaches itself to the person's psyche and could affect their emotions. Not knowing this, we go out and buy clothing and other gadgets for our children with negative connotations and expect them to behave in a good manner yet, we're the ones who dressed them up for the action!

Sometimes your favourite shop may sell certain types of attire in the sizes your children wear, yet consideration of the message they carry is crucial to the child's attitude. <u>Just as we consider carefully what goes into our stomach that may affect our well-being</u>, it is good to consider also what words we are feeding ourselves and our children. I'm not having a pop at parents (being one myself), but I realise now, having in the past bought clothes for my children because they look good or perhaps there was a bargain to be had that I did not pay much attention to the words I was buying into.

Consequently, the same goes for NAMES given to children; parents should ask – what is in a name? Names carry weight – good or bad! What we call our offspring is vital to their destiny!

Numerous parents seem to under-estimate the power and effect a name may have on their offspring. They may name them after a famous person or give them a name with a ring seemingly sounding good – perhaps the name of an ancestor. Some may not even check the meaning of the name they call their child or may not know whether the name is good or bad. I've known people who have changed the name they were given at birth, because it carried a negative vibe or it didn't do anything to make them feel good. I believe any names given should be good and purposeful!

We read in the Bible how Benjamin's mother had given him a negative name –Ben-oni, 'son of my sorrow'; but his father Jacob quickly changed it to **'son of my right hand'**!

Again, Jabez's mother also gave him the negative name which meant –'pain'. This name did not do anything to uplift him, so much so that he called upon Almighty God for help in this regard and his request was granted with favour, influence, abundance and protection. (1 Chron. 4 v 9-10).

## A PURPOSEFUL NAME
&lt;+&gt;
What's in a name? Some may ask;
Others only care when the meaning is unmasked!
A name could lift or pull you down
So choose and respect one that's profound!
Jesus, the name above all, we proclaim -
His, is universally famed
Yet, it bears no dread or ill
And is the sweetest, still!
From A-Z in the alphabet,
We describe his Deity yet;
Words may describe or say who He is,
But nothing compare to His gracious riches!
He, so highly exalted now -
His Name compels us to bow!
&lt;+&gt;

A-    AWESOME
B-    BELOVED
C-    CONQUEROR

D- DELIVERER
E- ETERNAL
F- FAITHFUL
G- GRACIOUS
H- HEALER
I- INFINITE
J- JUST
K- KING
L- LOYAL
M- MAJESTIC
N- NOBLE
O- OMNISCIENT
P- POWERFUL
Q- QUALIFIABLE
R- RULER
S- SAVIOUR
T- TEACHER
U- UNIVERSAL
V- VICTORIOUS
W- WORSHIPFUL
X- XENIAL
Y- YESHUA
Z- ZEALOUS

**(A good name is rather to be chosen than great riches**
... (Proverbs 22v1)

**(A good name is better than precious ointment ....**
(Ecclesiastes 7v1))

## CHAPTER 4

## LEADERS TOO NEED GOOD WORDS

Still leading on good words, Bible Scripture tells us that **prayers and giving of thanks should be made for all people;** for Heads of Government, (those in authority), and Kings (the Royal family) that we may lead a peaceable life in all godliness and honesty; **for this is good and acceptable** in the sight of God our Saviour, who desire all to be saved and to come unto the knowledge of the truth. (See 1 Timothy 2 v1-4).

Every Leader needs to know that their work and service is held in high esteem - Leaders are humans - **they too would appreciate good words).**

In honour of Her Majesty, the Queen I felt compelled to pen these words in celebration of her 'Diamond Jubilee' (2013), in recognition of her ardent work:

### The DIAMOND JUBILEE of Her Majesty, the QUEEN
~*~

All hail, your Royal Majesty, the Queen
And long may you live, we sing!
With joy we celebrate your 'Diamond Jubilee'

As an honour and precious legacy!
Your 60 years' reign deserves a tribute
And, to you Ma'am, we salute!
Young and tender you came to the throne,
Embracing dutiful tasks - you own;
Yet, with graceful diligence
Portraying qualities of excellence!
Head of the Commonwealth, Queen of England,
Head of State for the United Kingdom;
You provide links for law, history and culture,
A magnetic bridge to bring people together!

~*~

Whether the official opening of buildings and events,
Cheering heroes on their achievements;
Reviewing the troops or appreciating a war veteran,
You aptly fulfil your vocation!
You've gained the respect of the world;
This is more than a precious pearl!
As you travelled far and wide,
Millions revere you as a respectable guide;
You often promote family values,
Inspiring us, the best to choose!
Through your own challenges you've helped us learn
By your tenacity, as you stood firm;
Furthermore, as a mother and grandmother
You caringly kept your composure!

~*~

At such an auspicious time,
This calls for melody, rhythm and rhyme;
Great Britain and the world will celebrate
And, in this Jubilee event participate;

Church bells would be ringing
As prayers are uttered in thanksgiving!
There'll be street parties and parades,
Music and feasting until the night fades;
People will reflect, rejoice and dance
For this given privilege and chance;
A mark of respect is fitting for your reign -
To the throne, we're glad you came!
~*~
Your esteem Royal Highness,
You've dedicated yourself to a life of service,
You've served with dignity, loyalty and dedication
And we, your subjects extend to you, our hearty
congratulations!
~*~

**Good Words** could encourage a father who amidst life's challenging situations, desires to do his best for his family while keeping the family unit together – good Words like these: -

### A Gracious Father
~✦~
You are a gracious father
Who truly deserves an honour!

You bring joy to your family circle,
You're a sound and good role model!
Altogether your child's ideal,
A father transparent and real!
You shoulder your responsibility
Expressing care and loyalty!
For your child you give quality time,
Even join in their nursery rhyme!
You're a father very dear,
Any season of the year!

~❖~~*❖*~

## Father of Nations
~*❖*~

'Father of Nations', Abram
Left his home for another land!
Although he didn't understand,
He boldly obeyed God's command!
Defying his native choice,
He solely heeded God's voice
To come out from his country -
The place of his nativity!
God told him that his name would be great
And, of him a great nation he'd make!
Blessing upon blessings he'd conceive

For all people and their families!
Abram, his wife and Lot his brother's son,
Took their substance and travelled to Canaan;
The place where God appeared to Abram,
Affirming that he would give his seed this land!
There, he built an altar unto the Lord,
A token for the promised reward!
Travelling south he experienced famine,
Where in Egypt he sought food and lodging!
Leaving there he journeyed to Bethel,
When strife crept in where he did dwell;
He knew that he and Lot couldn't stay together,
As their herds men contended with each other;
Separating, Lot chose fertile Jordan,
Pitching his tent towards Sodom,
While Abram dwelt in Canaan!
Very soon, as if by surprise,
God said to him, "lift up now your eyes" -
From the place where you are northward,
South, East and Westward,
All the land you see altogether
Will I give you and your seed forever!

## BLESSED!

**\*\*+\*\***

**Truly 'Blessed', I am -**

By Divine grace from the Father's hand!
I'm 'Blessed' with a prosperous yield,
Whether I'm in the city or field!
\*\*₊\*\*

## Favour!
\*\*₊\*\*

I'm bestowed abundant 'Favour',
Provided by God, the Giver!
Daily I enjoy good dividend -
My source is the 'Living Fountain'!
\*\*₊\*\*

# CHAPTER 5

## **ASPECTS OF GOOD WORDS**

In qualifying **a good word**, I give below part of a descriptive list taken mainly from Bible Scripture. Where there's an asterisk *, I've given an example when the appropriate word is use to bring good results:

| The Powerful Word | The Quickening Word | The Piercing Word |
| The Blessed Word | The Discerning Word | The Beginning Word* |
| The Rich Word* | The Fulfilling Word | The Loving Word |
| The Pure Word | The Eternal Word | The Illuminable Word* |
| The Fitting Word | The Healthy Word* | The Righteous Word |
| The Glorious Word | The Good Word* | The Enlightening Word |
| The Spiritual Word | The Healing Word* | The Cheerful Word* |
| The Glad Word* | The Living Word* | The Acceptable Word |

| | | |
|---|---|---|
| The True Word* | The Joyful Word* | The Cleansing Word* |
| The Pure Word | The Affirming Word | The Seasoned Word |
| The Fruitful Word | The Edifying Word | The Magnificent Word |
| The Sweet Word | The Pleasant Word | The Prosperous Word* |
| The Graceful Word | The Right Word | The Commendable Word |
| The Hopeful Word* | The Favoured Word | The Empowering Word |
| The Building Word | The Peaceful Word | The Accomplished Word* |
| The Proceeding Word* | The Excellent Word | The Prophetic Word |
| The Holy Word | The Confident Word | The Encouraging Word |
| The Precious Word | The Diligent Word | The Transforming Word |

| The Wise Word | The Wholesome Word | The Inspirational Word |
|---|---|---|
| The Wonderful Word | The Interesting Word | The Delivering Word |
| The Prevalent Word | The Honourable Word | The Saturating Word |
| The Enduring Word | The Revealing Word | The Compassionate Word |
| The Amazing Word* | The Marvellous Word* | The Faith-filled Word* |

- Jesus' spoke a **word of Amazement*** at the time when he awaken Jairus' daughter; so much so that she got up and walk, causing the people present to be **amazed**. (See St Mark 5v42).

... "**Be of good cheer, daughter; your faith has made you well**"... (St Matthew 9v22) was the '**Cheerful Word**'* which Jesus spoke to the woman who had a blood disease for 12 years.

- The '**Marvellous Word**'*: Jesus spoke and caused the tempest of the sea to obey him with the effect of calm.

Because of this, the men that were present **marvelled** at the obedience of the sea. (See St. Matthew 8v27).

- After Jesus healed the paralytic man; as recorded in St Matthew Chapter 9 verse 2; Jesus further heartens his spirit by giving him a **'good word'\***; he said to him, *"**Son, be of <u>good cheer</u> ...**"*

- In the **Beginning\*** of creation, darkness was upon the whole earth. Almighty God, the Creator, <u>spoke the very first good words</u> **to bring the universe into being!** Then God said, *"**Let there be light**"* **and there was light.** (Genesis 1v3).

- The **'Hopeful Word'\*** - Martin Luther King's moving speech in Washington DC - *"<u>I have a dream</u>"* is hailed as one of the most moving speeches ever spoken by a man: – *"I have a dream that my four little children will one day live in a nation where they will not be judged by the colour of their skin, but by the conduct of their character. I have a dream. I have a dream that one day in Alabama, with its vicious racists – one day right there in Alabama, little black boys and black girls will be able to join hands with* *little white boys and little white girls as brothers and sisters. I have a dream today"*.

In this moving inspirational message, he gave hope to millions of Americans, young and old. His '**Hopeful Words**'* still motivate Americans and those of African heritage. Even today, after more than 50 years on, Martin Luther King still inspires. (Some deem his speech – '17 minutes that changed the world forever')!

Martin Luther King gave hope that, one day people of African heritage would not be judged by the colour of their skin, but they like any other would be seen as making significant differences to their world. Decades later, the reality came when President Obama was elected the first Afro-American President on 21 January 2009.

-The '**Rich Word**'* – the people of Colossae were encouraged by Apostle Paul with these words; **Let the word of Christ dwell in you richly in all wisdom, teaching and admonishing one another in psalms and hymns and spiritual songs, singing with grace in your hearts to the Lord.** (Colossians 3v16).

-The '**Illuminable Word**'* - David, the Shepherd boy

who later was crowned King so loved and respected the word of God that he asserts; - **The entrance of your word gives light; it gives understanding to the simple.** (Psalms 119v130).

-The **'Proceeding Word'\*/'Living Word'\*** - Jesus stood up against the Devil when he tempted him to turn stones into bread, after Jesus had fasted forty days; Jesus rebuked the Devil and pointed out that: ...**'Man shall not live by bread alone, but by every word that proceeds from the mouth of God';** (St Matthew 4v4); affirming that the living bread of God's word is superior to the temporal bread.

-The **'Accomplished\*/ Prosperous\* Word'**: - In the Book of Isaiah 55, we see that Almighty God calls everyone to faith and repentance and to turn away from wickedness and He will abundantly pardon. Furthermore, He promises peace, fruitfulness, and prosperity; verifying this in verse 11; - "... **So shall My word be that goes forth from my mouth; it shall not return to Me void, but it shall accomplish what I please, and it shall prosper in the thing for which I sent it. ...".** (Isaiah. 55v10-11).

-The **'Healthy Word'*** - Solomon, the wisest man who ever lived proved that the words of Almighty God provides health. In one of his numerous 'nuggets of wisdom' Solomon affirms that; **Pleasant words are like a honeycomb, Sweetness to the soul and health to the bones.** (Proverbs 16v24).

-The **'Joyful Word'*** - I believe when you internalise good words, you become a product of good words and their effect is seen in your characteristics. Jeremiah seemed to fit this criterion as he asserts this of God's Word: **Your words were found, and I ate them and your word was to me, the joy and rejoicing of my heart..;** (Jeremiah 15v16).

-The **'Living Word'*** - during Jesus' ministry here on earth, one day he was explaining to the people by the seaside about the words of life which he spoke and the difference between the temporal and the spiritual bread; He said that; **'It is the Spirit who gives life; the flesh profits nothing; the words that I speak to you they are Spirit and they are life.**(St John 6v63).

-The **'True Word'*** - Abraham, the father of many nations, (See Genesis 17v4); in faith, believed the true and powerful words of God that He would give him a son; (Abraham was 99 years old then). Although this was fulfilled some 13 years later, the world knows that the nation of Israel is the blood descendants of Abraham.

**Good Words** are like a medicine! People mostly act on good words that they believe would benefit them. I was in the Supermarket the other day when I heard this smartly-dressed lady muttering these words to herself; "I'm sure she said it was the tea in a green box that would help lower blood pressure ...." while she continued combing the shop shelf for her tea. A friend had told her about this healthy tea, she assured me, when I asked her concerning the tea. (I conclude that the **Healthy Word*** spoken to this lady caused her to act and pursue a health- giving product). No wonder the word in Scripture says, **Pleasant words are like a honeycomb, Sweetness to the soul and health to the bones** (Prov. 16v24).

The following **Commendable Words*** were spoken to the believers at Ephesus by the Apostle Paul in his closing speech, before taking his journey to Jerusalem: **"So now, brethren, I commend you to God and to the word of His grace, which is able to build you up and** *give you an inheritance among all those who are sanctified"*. (Acts 20v32). (Paul gave them this gift of good words which he affirms would bring them into prominence, producing the wealth of an inheritance and eternal blessings).

In the book of St John 3v16-17, Jesus declares the **'Loving Word'\*** : - These are the profound loving words from our Heavenly Father - *For God so loved the world that He gave His only begotten Son, that whoever believes in Him should not perish but have everlasting life. For God did not send His Son into the world to condemn the world, but that the world through him might be saved.*

## Pursue 'Good Words'

Simon Peter **pursued Jesus** because of his profound words throughout his teaching ministry. One day, when Jesus asked Peter and the other disciples whether they would go away and leave him, Peter exclaimed; "Lord, to whom shall we go? You have the words of eternal life".

(See St John 6v68-69). Consequently, Jesus explained to the people listening to his sermon that the words he spoke to them are Spirit and Life.

King David testified that God's words are more to be desired than gold, yes, than much fine gold; sweeter also than honey and the honeycomb; (See Psalms 19v10). He internalised these good words to such an extent that their effect were priceless, in his estimation.

### CHOSEN!
**+**

**Born for greatness and 'chosen',
I'm uniquely one in a million!
Divinely connected and faith-driven,
I'm an heir of the 'Heavenly Kingdom'!**
**+**

**An invitation from a good person** should bring joy to those invited: the Lord God caused Prophet Isaiah to pen this invitation to one and all — "Look unto me and be saved, all you ends of the earth! For I am God and there is no other". (Isaiah 45 v 22).

__Good words are not to be despised__: The writer of Proverbs warns: He who despises the word will be destroyed, but he who fears the commandments will be rewarded. (Proverbs 13v13).

__Good words are sought after__: Kings and Leaders in ancient times sought out prophets and godly people to enquire whether there were any words from the Lord, especially if they were going into battle or if they were sick.

King Zedekiah had disobeyed and forsaken the Lord, yet sent and took the Prophet Jeremiah out of prison and asked him secretly whether there was any word from the Lord; however, Jeremiah gave him a word of truth from the Lord; ... Jeremiah said, ... "You shall be delivered into the hand of the King of Babylon!" (See Jeremiah 37v 17).

Another king, Ahaziah; who had fallen through the lattice of his upper chamber and took sick; after seeking advice from evil sources, eventually made enquiry of the Prophet of God for a **good word**, whether he would recover of his illness or not. (See 2Kings 1-18).

A faith-filled inspirational poem:

### **HEALING for YOU!**
**\*\*+\*\***

You need not stand in a queue –
'I am the Lord that heals you' -
Is Jesus' assurance still new!
Believe Him with all your heart,
Call on His name for a start;
He'll give you His inner peace
And full joy in your soul release!
**\*\*+\*\***

A Roman Centurion who had great respect for Jesus' **profound words** and power, turned to Jesus for help; so much so that, when his servant took sick, he made a request for Jesus to come to his house and heal his servant but, soon afterwards, he decided to send another message saying to Jesus: ... **"Say the word, and my servant will be healed ..."**; (See St Luke 7v2-10) - The Centurion knew that Jesus had the **Healing Word!**

## The Centurion's Faith
+❖+
A man of great faith was that Centurion
Who heard that Jesus was at Capernaum?

His servant was sick, so he could not delay,
For his servant needed a miracle that very day!
+❖+
Hastily he sent a message to the Jews
Who could not in any way his request refuse;
A favour of Jesus they dared not dismiss,
He was worthy for whom Jesus should do this!
The Jews approached Jesus on him to rely,
To heal the servant who was ready to die,
So off Jesus went to show his compassion
And perhaps meet the great Centurion!
+❖+
But the Centurion's faith was beyond compare;
He believed in healing without Jesus being there,
He sent friends to Jesus saying, 'trouble not yourself'
For he believed the servant had recovered his health!
He said, 'I'm not worthy that you should come under my roof -
The Centurion knew already that he had the proof;
As he exercised his faith all would be revealed
And Jesus only need say so, and his servant be healed!
+❖+
~❖~~❖~~❖~~❖~

# CHAPTER 6

## 'GOOD WORDS COULD WORK FOR YOU!

! Good Words could build confidence;

! Good Words could reverse an adverse situation.

! Good Words could prevent strife;

! Good Words bring comfort;

! Good Words could invoke a reward;

! Good Words may provide a needed antidote;

! Good Words help relieve stress;

! Good Words bring a change for the better;

! Good Words open doors of opportunity;

! Good Words draw multitudes to listen;

! Good Words elevates people;

! Good Words are remembered;

! Good Words build emotional bridges!

## Seeds of good words are compelling!

The seeds of good words which Jesus spoke during his time here on earth attracted multitudes of people to hear him. Numerous people who were unhappy or stressed, heard him say, 'Blessed are the poor in spirit, for theirs is the kingdom of heaven'; again, 'Blessed are they that mourn for they shall be comforted' …..! (Matthew 5 v 1-12).

## Good Words should be acted upon!

**The People at Berea, having heard good words from the disciples, decided to go home and search the Scriptures daily for themselves.** No doubt, they received further knowledge and empowerment for edification. (See Acts 17 v 10-11).

## There's a reward for good words!

Caleb was rewarded by God for the good report that he brought back from the land of giants- he was among those who entered 'the Promised Land'. Some others in his company who spoke adverse words when they made their presentation to Moses were barred from entering 'the Promised Land'. (See Numbers. 14v20-24).

## Good Words bring reconciliation!

The people at Corinth heard from the Apostle Paul the good words of God's love for them and the whole world; how that in forgiving their trespasses, He through Christ Jesus had committed unto us the **word of reconciliation.** (See 2 Corinthians 5 v 19).

Unusual, influential and profound words will cause the hearers to marvel and make comments (as was the case throughout Jesus' ministry). One of such times was when he cast out an unclean spirit from a man; those standing by exclaimed – **"what a word is this"!** (See St Luke 4v36).

## GOOD WORDS ARE EFFECTIVE, ESPECIALLY WHEN THEY ARE TIMELY!

✯ ❖ ✯

**Anxiety in the heart of man causes depression, but a good word makes it glad.** (Proverbs.12v25).

✯ ❖ ✯

**A word fitly spoken is like apples of gold in pictures**

*of silver.* (Proverbs 25v11).

*Pleasant words are like a honeycomb, sweetness to the soul and health to the bones.* (Proverbs 16 v 24).

*Good words from Jesus brings cleansing – (inner cleansing), as he told his disciples.* (See St. John 15v3).

A good invitation is mostly always accepted especially, if it is to one's benefit – 'The good news of Salvation' (deliverance) is profoundly so:

### SALVATION CALLS

To you Salvation now calls –
"Come and be saved, one and all"!
It's today, not tomorrow,
You can't hours from yesterday borrow!
It's not if, but when –
Summer's ended, the harvest is past; what then?

You say, "I have time,
There's a queue, I must wait in line";
"At least, I have an excuse –
What have I got to lose"?
"Hey, I'm still a child,
I'll stay and play for a while"!

2-

Salvation still beckons
To your life and time, it reckons –
"Remember your Creator while you're still young,
Embrace Him in your heart; He'll not let you down!
While the sun shines upon your youth
You follow your heart's desires in truth;
Remember that God will judge you
For all and whatever you do;
While the light of the moon be not darkened,
Take heed to 'Salvation's call', please hearken!

3-

Growing up you say, "I have a career to pursue
And check out friends, old and new;
I must travel; the world I must see,
There's so much pleasure out there for me"!
Salvation says, "hurry and come";
You say, "I'm having great fun;

I've just married a wife,
She's the sweet fragrance of my life;
My kids I need to educate –
I can't my responsibility forsake"?
Salvation warns, "the end is drawing near",
You quibbled, "what did you say"?
"I'm too busy with a potential job prospect,
I can't this opportunity reject;
Money is in my eye to gather;
Promotion's in view, I must climb the ladder"!

4-

Again, Salvation says, "come and be saved,
The end is not only death and the grave;
Bodies will return to earth's dust;
Breath returns to God who gave it, is must!
Jesus gave his life to save you from sin
Offering you life everlasting"!
You say, "I'll come as soon as I retire –
No point being stuck in sin's mire"!

5-

Eventually, you become sick –
You say, "I'll call the doctor quick;
I'll stay off work - this is my ploy?
My life, I do not now enjoy"!

Your hair starts turning white;
You develop poor eyesight;
Your arms begin to tremble;
Legs that were strong cause you now to tumble;
Your teeth falls out - one, then a few,
Making it difficult your food to chew;
Your eyes grow dim day by day;
The noise in the street you can barely hear
As songs of sweet music play;
A final resting place upon your thoughts fall –
What then, would you say to 'Salvation's call"?

## CHAPTER 7

### A KING'S PERSPECTIVE ON 'GOOD WORDS'

The Psalmist, King David esteem God's Word above food, drink, pleasure and even his very existence! He was one of the most successful Kings ever lived. It is recorded that he was a man after God's own heart; (See Acts 13v22; 1 Sam. 13v14). He relied on God for help even in his communication; he said to God; - **Let the words of my mouth and the meditation of my heart be acceptable in Your sight, O LORD, my strength and my Redeemer.** (Psalms 19 v14).

As we read of King David's life in the Books of Samuel, Kings, Chronicles and Psalms, we would understand the reason for his greatness. Below is a selection of declarations of what he had to say about God's word and its usage:

- **as a sin buffer:** Your word I have hidden in mine heart that I might not sin against you (Psalms 119v11).

- **as a lantern:** Your word is a lamp to my feet and a light to my path (Psalms 119v105).

- **as a teacher:** the entrance of Your word gives light; it gives understanding to the simple (Psalms 119v130).

- **as a path director**: Direct my steps by Your word, and let no iniquity have dominion over me (Psalms 119v133).

- **as a spiritual cleanser:** how can a young man cleanse his way? By taking heed according to Your word (Psalms 119 v 9).

Furthermore, the Psalmist and King, David, in encouraging the people to rejoice and praise the Lord with a new song and musical instruments, he declared: that; **For the LORD is righteous; He loves righteousness; His countenance beholds the upright.** (Psalms 11v7).

Good words shape character:

Good character is paramount in anyone's life; especially that of a young person. Perhaps, that's why the Psalmist asked the question; 'how can a young man cleanse his way'? This searching question in Psalms 119 verse 9 is immediately followed by the fitting reply from the same text; 'By taking heed according to Your word.

Furthermore, the first verse of Ecclesiastes 12 verse 1 admonished the young thus; **Remember now your**

*Creator in the days of your youth, before the difficult days come and the years draw near when you say, "I have no pleasure in them".*

Moreover, a wealth of good instruction on how to gain wisdom and knowledge is found in the Book of Proverbs, in the quest to honour Almighty God.

# CHAPTER 8

## ILL/INAPPROPRIATE WORDS COULD BE WOUNDING

After highly recommending good and profound words, it would be wrong for me not to present, for the sake of comparison, examples of bad, ill or inappropriate words. Most people may accept that ill or profane words do not build up or edify anyone; neither do inappropriate words lift anyone's spirit at any time, especially if they are feeling stressed or under the weather - so to speak.

*A man who bears false witness against his neighbour is like a club, a sword and a sharp arrow!* (Proverbs 25v18).

*He who goes about as a tale bearer reveals secrets, therefore do not associate with one who flatters with his lips!* (Proverbs 20v19).

*A fool's lips enter contention and his mouth calls for blows!* (Proverbs 18v6).

*Getting treasures by a lying tongue is the fleeting fantasy of those who seek death!* (Proverbs 21v6).

*A whisperer separates the best of friends!* (Proverbs

*16v28)*

Inappropriate words do not promote health or bring hope. This instruction Paul, the Apostle gave to young Timothy, his protégé: ... **But shun profane and idle babblings, for they will increase to more ungodliness.** (See 2 Timothy 2v16).

Consider the following scenarios:

Should I know someone who is ailing; suffering with severe stomach pains and had decided to visit them and, in conversation, I announced that I heard on 'the News' this morning that a few people with stomach pains died on their way to hospital. I'm sure I would not have lifted that person's spirit in any way? My insensitive words may have caused this person to collapse with shock?

Again, should there be a budding entrepreneur by the name of Mr McLean who had been made redundant from his job and had decided to set up a 'dry cleaning business' in his local area because he saw it as a good business opportunity as there were no such services there.

On the day of opening, a certain Mr Doubty came into the shop and announced, "Boy, what do you think you are doing"? "I can't see you succeeding at this cleaning business at all, people round here don't like spending money on things like dry cleaning; haven't you heard about the economic downturn"? (With such negative words, I believe that Mr Doubty had not been encouraging whatsoever, but he may have dampened Mr McLean's optimism)!

A child attending a Junior High School, one day excitedly ran to her mother and announced, "Mum, I got top marks in Biology today, and my teacher says that I could become a Doctor"! Immediately, her mother remarked, "you can forget about that, I have no money to put you through Med School and besides, no one in our family has ever been a doctor"! Upon hearing this, the child ran upstairs to her room in tears, **her confidence being crushed** by her mother's negative words! **(This mother had failed to consider the power of her words on the destiny of her child;** – *Death and life are in the power of the tongue* and those who love it will eat its fruit. (Proverbs 18v21).

## The words of Leaders' should be honourable

It is a fact that many people look-up to the rich, powerful and famous for their queue. Some like politicians may make promissory speeches while campaigning during election time and may never deliver what they promise if they are elected to government.

While visiting a certain country and walking along a grass land that was familiar to me, (which once had a pavilion erected for young people to watch football), I enquired from my acquaintance that was travelling with me what had become of the wooden pavilion. I was informed that the Politician for that constituency had promised the young people in that area a new pavilion while he was campaigning; however, it was now some <u>7 years since that promise was made and the new pavilion had not materialised</u>.

The above is one example only, but thousand could say it is true that, during a country's election campaign, they would hear people murmuring of the broken promises of people in power – (I've heard some of it myself) - It would appear then that all words spoken by influential people **are not always good**!

Countless people would perhaps like to be a fly on the wall in the corridors of power where the Politicians make decisions that affect the lives of constituents. More importantly, leaders of nations have a duty **to uphold the meaningful words** they convey to the people whom they represent; especially as Bible Scripture tells that **the seat of power is established in righteousness**.

Several years ago, it was told that some politicians in a US State had a rude awakening when they invited a certain Preacher to initiate the opening prayer at one of their events. The Preacher, being led by the words from Isaiah chapter 5 verses 20; beginning thus:

**"Woe to those who call evil good and good evil; who put darkness for light and light for darkness; who put bitter for sweet and sweet for bitter ..."**

I read that this caused a great stir that day amongst

those who were in the audience listening and that some were shuffling in their seats! However, I deem that the prayer served as a reminder to the Leaders of their duty! Nevertheless, the Preacher was acting in the capacity of his profession - reminding the hearers of the words of Almighty God).

I note from the 3rd Epistle of St John,; that the Apostle St John warns Gaius of Diotrephes, a brother, who used malicious words against them. St John, furthermore admonishes Gaius, do **not imitate what is evil but what is good.** ... (See 3rd John v 9-11).

- We could concur then that, malicious words do not build up anyone!

Again, Brother Jude in his Epistle; (See verse 16); warns of grumblers, complainers and **those whose mouth speak great swelling words, flattering people to gain advantage.** It would appear that these people did not use their mouths to benefit others, but ill only!

**Let no corrupt word proceed from your mouth, but**

***what is good for necessary edification, that it may impart grace to the hearers.*** (Ephesians 4v29).

Halloween celebration (which was meant to celebrate the end of Harvest) has become a big trend world-wide and growing each year. We see children and adults dressed up in various types of Witch and Wizards' outfit going from house to house, knocking on doors and announcing the words,' **trick or treat'.** While some children enjoy doing this because, many come away from the exercise with plenty of sweets and sometimes, even cash. On the other hand, this event could turn sour if children misuse this privilege. There have been shameful nuisances surrounding the event when some children threw eggs upon residents' homes when they didn't receive a treat. I've witnessed egg residue on doors and door steps the morning after Halloween. **(This appalling act is unacceptable and brings negative results rather than good. Furthermore there is no hope for the children or anyone in the indulgence of Halloween).**

Moreover, I've heard reports from the media that some

children go missing during the Halloween period. (In this type of exercise it is true to say that there are no guarantees that the door which children knock on, the person living therein has good intentions. Although it is meant for fun, I deem this exercise unsafe for children without adult supervision).

There is an event that could be enjoyable for everyone – Christmas! Its root word is 'Christ' – Christ Jesus who came with GOOD NEWS and hope for all people; this poem speaks about Christmas from Heaven's point of view:

## **Christmas from Heaven's point of view**

**The Christmas story is old, yet still very new –
A phenomenal reality, undoubtedly true
That, a heavenly King was born
To live in human hearts; them to reform!**

**Yet, God meant it a time of goodwill,
Of joy and cheer our spirit to fill;
So Christ Jesus is that eternal bliss,
A daily present and life-long gift!**

A life of sharing God meant this to be
That we should show Love to the needy
Reaching out to the lonely and poor
And show Christ-likeness more and more!

"Emmanuel – God with us", we believe;
In faith we embrace this and it receive!
This promise is to all, the Scripture says
By the 'Prince of Peace' who dispel our fears!

He's the Wonderful Counsellor and Saviour,
The Mighty God and Everlasting Father -
Who came to save all people from sin
Giving them hope and Eternal Life to win!

Whatever people's heart may yearn?
Or to what they may give concern,
I submit to you this –
That Christ Jesus is still the 'perfect gift'
Beyond what anyone might wish!
So let's celebrate with joy and thanksgiving,
Praising God with the host of Heaven!

I pose now a scenario case where I have asked some Bible characters to speak for themselves as I present the case of:

### Mr Goodman versus Mr Negative
<<*>>

It was alleged that a certain Mr Goodman, a local youth club Manager, was in the market-place promoting an initiative called 'possibility youths' when, Mr Negative, an acquaintance of Mr G; who was passing that way, abruptly interrupted Mr 'G'; pointing his finger in his face, pushing him to the ground and assaulting him while throwing a few choice  - claiming that, "no one round here is up for change; what good is a youth initiative? Youths need money, not talk". (However, the case was eventually brought before the Crown Court).

The Judge, in his opening remarks used a quotation from the Book of Proverbs in addressing the court!

He then turn to the Prosecution to present the case, adding that in due course the 'Defendant' and the 'Plaintiff' will be called accordingly and that witnesses also will be called to the stand to give evidence.

The Prosecution in summary highlighted that there is the Indictment which carries the 'Statement of Offence' and the 'Particulars of Offence', along with the 'case bundle' to consider. The case proceeded.

Mr Negative was called to the stand; he feebly scrambled to his feet trying to gain momentum; blurted out: "what is this all about though? "Cursing don't hurt anyone; lots of people use the 'F' word, that is the trend; besides, I can't see any good coming from what Mr 'G' is trying to make the youths believe - no point looking for jobs in this recession - things will only get worse for the youths"……(Mr Negative then starts mumbling, …..).

Mr 'G' was called to the stand; (he, walking confidently); stated that he is willing to forgive Mr 'N' and stressed that **positive words are uplifting** and **invaluable** in **boosting the confidence** of young people, especially in the current climate of the famine for decent words. He added that, "G**ood will always triumph the over bad**"! Furthermore, Mr Goodman affirmed that the apprenticeship scheme would benefit Mr Negative also'.

Mr Goodman further said, "I would like now to call some witnesses who would enlighten Mr Negative with good positive words from scripture texts and I hope that Mr 'N' would be inspired by them".

Mr 'G' called the following:

**King Solomon; Prophet Nahum; Prophet Isaiah; King David and Jesus – King of Kings!**

## Solomon

(Solomon decked in gold attire from head to toe); anxious to impart some of his wisdom into the young man's spirit, spoke assuredly to Mr 'N' thus:

*You are snared by the words of your mouth; you are taken by the words of your mouth. So do this, my son, and deliver yourself; for you have come into the hand of your friend, go and humble yourself; plead with your friend.* (Proverbs 6v2-3).

*Do not be wise in your own eyes; fear the LORD and depart from evil. It will be health to your flesh, and strength to your bones.* (Proverbs 3 v 7-8).

## Nahum

(Nahum briskly entered) and declared:

*The LORD is good, a stronghold in the day of trouble; and He knows those who trust in Him.* (Nahum 1 v7).

## Isaiah

(Isaiah, girded with a suitably fitted mantel), confidently spoke:

*The Lord GOD has given Me the tongue of the*

*learned, that I should know how to speak a word in season to him who is weary...* (Isaiah 50 v 4). (Thus Isaiah continued his advice with encouraging words to Mr N).

## David

(Enter David – leaning on his rod and staff and duly delivered his speech) -:

*...For the word of the LORD is right and all His works is done in truth.* (Psalms 33 v 4).

Asking Mr N a question and giving him the answer, King David said, *"How can a young man cleanse his ways? By taking heed according to Your word.* (Psalms 119 v 9).

## Jesus

(Wearing a distinctive coat woven from top to bottom, entered with coolness and an air of authority, so much so that the ambience of his presence lit up the court room – there was a certain stillness in the atmosphere); Jesus spoke on this wise:

... *"It is written, 'Man shall not live by bread alone, but by every word that proceeds from the mouth of God'".* (Matthew 4v4) *... the words that I speak to you, are spirit and they are life.* (St John 6v63) - (affirming that humans need God, their maker, in order for them to live wholesome lives).

In summary, the Judge thanked everyone and commended Mr 'G' for his work in bringing an initiative to support and motivate the youths. He commended him also for forgiving Mr 'Negative' and dropping all charges against him. Furthermore, he commended Mr 'Goodman' for offering an apprenticeship opportunity to Mr 'N'.

The case was dismissed as the court erupted into a rapturous applaud!

## SOLOMON

A man of excellent wisdom
Was Israel's King Solomon;
Visited by God in a dream
For to grant him a wish supreme;
He did not ask for tons of gold,
Honour or riches untold;
Neither did he desire a wicked thing
Like the death of an enemy!
He did not express a wish to live long
And be eternally strong,
But he had a good desire of heart -

One that sets him apart;
He ask for Wisdom and Knowledge
To judge rightly, his tasks envisage!

Because Solomon had passed God's test,
His reward was absolutely priceless!
There was no king the same as he,
Neither will there ever be!
Surpassing all Kings in riches and skill -
His wealth of Wisdom remains still!
You may desire to catch some in Ecclesiastes
And, in Proverbs, there're plenty of these!
Yet, there's the 'Song of Songs',
If for love your heart still longs!
Should you be given an uncommon wish;
Would yours ever top this?

## CHAPTER 9

## **THE CONSEQUENCE OF WORDS**

Some advertising agencies use billboards, placards, posters and other type of advertising to announce their trade. However, there are several of these that pounce on our sight and are especially offensive when they send out ill messages.

A Negative kind of word in motion is one aspect that gives me cause for some concern particularly, when I see graphic obscenity expressed in the public domain which sends out negative vibes, especially to young children!

I congratulate the young mother who led a campaign against supermarkets that were displaying at the front of their shops magazines and newspapers whose headlines contain inappropriate words and images that could harm the perception of young children. She argued that while she was out shopping with her young son, she did not want him to be subjected to having to read or see things that would distort his thinking. I applaud the supermarkets that complied with the wishes of this concerned young mother.

Word pictures can speak volumes to a person's emotion and could provoke/effect one's thought pattern in a good or bad way. It is fair to say that everyone is <u>affected in some way by songs and music</u> and what <u>they watch on the television, video, internet, mobile phones and other new technology</u>. I pray that God would use the same medium to highlight and confirm his power and grace unto Salvation through Jesus Christ - **the answer to all human fulfilment**.

As I was listening to the evening news I heard that the young man who had gunned down several pupils and teachers from his old primary school in the USA in November 2012 had been watching movies about killing, over and over again.

Prevalent in our world, is a flood of offensive graphic material which form parts of new technological games geared towards young people. These have greatly influenced their desire to want always to be engaged in playing games. It's very hard to engage in a meaningful conversation with young people these days when they're so mesmerised by these play station games.

I couldn't help but notice that amongst some

advertisements, there are on-line gambling which could potentially entice children to gamble and could lead them along the wrong path; however, the onus would be on the parents and their monitoring of their child's viewing. In saying that, the young generation seems to spend the majority of their time on the Internet, so it would be up to their own discretion to choose wisely with some good guidance.

While travelling by train some time ago I saw a billboard advertisement which said, "HOW TO GET AWAY WITH MURDER ..."! How distasteful, I thought! Whether the advertisement was meant to draw consumers to a particular product, or whether the pun was used to make one smile, I thought it had an evil connotation – (not everyone is familiar with certain English pun), so "how to get away with murder" could be taken literally in the crime-prevalent climate that we're living in. I believe that those evil words would not help to promote righteousness to people of any society!

Nonetheless, **there are still some good word pictures** for the eyes to feast on in some public places. I was passing through a market some time ago when I spotted one or two stalls bearing pictures in shape of words that said:

☆ THANKS!

☆ WELCOME!

☆ HAVE A NICE DAY!

☆ JOY BRINGS A WELL NEEDED TONIC TO BODY AND SOUL IN ANY CLIMATE!

☆ FAITH LOOKS UP TO HOPE!

☆ RUN TO WIN; and

Other positive quotes!

## RUN WELL

<<>+<>>

It's not how you begin,

But if you run to win!

We pass this way once only -

**To make good use of time is our duty -**

**Life prevents a rehearsal;**

**It urges, "Come now and be full"!**

**When all is said and done**

**At the 'setting of the sun',**

**Will you receive an accolade?**

**For some achievements made?**

**Will you carry a beacon or ensign?**

**When you cross the 'Finish Line'?**

<+>

More significantly, the Bible tells us that Jesus Christ **(the Living Word)** was sacrificed for our sins on a Cross. As He was nailed to the cross, this scene, no doubt, provoked different types of opinion from those who watched or pass by. **He was like a picture of wonder!** Yet, he was a person who went about doing good – aiding the poor, healing the sick, feeding the hungry and teaching people how to live godly.

However, **with profound** good words, Jesus forgave those who beat him to death!  Jesus cried from the cross and prayed to God, ... ***"Father forgive them, for they do not know what they do"...*** (See St Luke 23 verse 34).

A person who emulated the forgiveness of Jesus Christ was the late, Nelson Mandela, the late president of South Africa - the world is well familiar with his phenomenal story how, he as a civil rights leader for the people of South Africa, was put in prison for many years and suffered much hardship. Subsequently, he forgave his captors and the Apartheid movement, **encouraging and motivating the people of South Africa with positively good words.** He went on to become President of South Africa, and received a Nobel Peace Prize. He led his people with much dignity and enthusiasm – one of his quotes goes like this: **'*It is better to lead from behind and to put others in front, especially when you celebrate victory when nice things occur. You take the front line when there is danger. Then people will appreciate your leadership*'** – this is a leader to emulate!

# CHAPTER 10

## SPEAK 'GOOD WORDS' INTO YOUR OWN LIFE!

There are times when one needs **to speak good positive words into their own lives!** Good words will also cause a woman of any age to know they are valued and that they could be virtuous. It would urge them to evaluate who they are; would encourage them not to sell themselves short, but could inspire them to demonstrate their God-given potential.

Here, this poem expresses the visionary words that I've spoken into my life – (I pray that those **who love good words** would pursue their dreams and find their own forte in life and be a blessing to their world):

*Charm is deceptive and beauty is passing, but a woman who fears the LORD, she shall be praised.*
(Proverbs 31 v 30)

### THE FULFILLED WOMAN
*~◊~*

**(This alludes to the truly virtuous woman)**
*~◊~*

A woman of profound vision I am,
Uniquely designed by God, the Father's hand;

One of notable character,
Responsible, courageous and a hard worker!
I'm created for maximum success,
Being endowed with seeds of greatness!
*~◇~*
Living by Faith I see the invisible
Endowed with Wisdom from His divine oracle;
Inspired creativity stirs my vision,
Aiding my goals to resourceful fruition!
My blessed intuition keeps me focussed -
Disciplined and creative, I'm industrious!
I'm conscientious, dependable and strong,
Confident that Christ is my Strength and Song!
*~◇~*
Attention to detail I strictly give,
Diligent in business, I'm intuitive;
Offering compliments without jealousy;
Easily forgiving people, quickly!
Prayer is my vital daily communion
With Father, Son and Holy Spirit in union;
As my heart ignites powerful praise,
In spiritual zest my voice I raise!
*~◇~*
I'm also a woman of prized value,
One of Honour and classy too!
My magnetic qualities are enshrined
By the characteristics of Christ, the Divine!

I'm generous, caring and compassionate;
With empathy, the broken I comfort!
In Love I speak words of wisdom,
Stirring hearers with enthusiasm!
*~◇~*

Cheerfully, I aid the poor,
Not looking for a reward, yet it is sure!
I experience a life of joy and prosperity,
Bounded by Peace as I walk in victory!
By apt discretion, I'm trustworthy,
Portraying the beautiful spirit of humility!
I have a sure harbour in which to hope,
One which the enemy cannot revoke!
*~◇~*

I'll never sell myself short
For my gifted potential has been uncorked
To make talented discoveries -
For in me, there're plenty of these!
*~◇~*

Our Conduct, Conversation and Character speak volumes and the goodness we demonstrate are imperative to our way of life; therefore, our brother and Apostle, Peter reminds believers in Christ that, we are 'Royalty'... (See 1 Peter 2 v 9). The Bible further allude to this in other places; e.g. Psalms 47v6-7; *Sing praises to God, sing praises; sing praises to our King, sing praises! For God is the King of all the earth ...*

(I deem that I'm included among the countless daughters of the <u>King of Kings</u> and the Lords of Lords – Almighty God).

Whilst reading a Psalm about the King's daughter, I was inspired with this poem:-

### The King's Daughter
~*+*~

The King's daughter is glorious within,
Blood-bought and liberated from sin;
She's an ambassador of Heaven,
One of a kind and chosen!
Her King gave His life, her to redeem,
That hers should be abundant and supreme!
Each day she steps out in majesty
Being assured of her destiny!
Her attire is 'the Gold of Righteousness',
Her head bears 'the Crown' of Salvation's goodness;
She wears a precious glow upon her face -
A reflection of the King's special Grace;
In her regal walk this is clear to see,
That the 'Fruit of Love' enhances her beauty!
Her character reflects the Kingdom's protocol;

Keeping its principles, she walks tall
With much dignity and ambient flare
In 'the elegance of Meekness' without a care;
Evil gossips her spirit annoys
As purity of heart gives her much joy,
For her thoughts are towards Heaven
The place of the eternal Jerusalem!

~*+*~

There are some 'Celebrities' who honour others by way of their vocation; motivating and appreciating people during their television programmes. Such a person is Ophra Winfrey who spoke good words in her own life and encouraged others to see the good in themselves; that they have value and usefulness in life. I pen this poem in honour of Ophra after I heard that her regular programme was going off the air:-

## Ophra - an Icon
*~◇~*

The day appeared uncertain;
It seemed like the final curtain
Drawn on your TV show
Where good values of life you'd explore
And showcase these to rich and poor;
For many you'd been a great mentor;
For others, a dynamic motivator

Touching hearts from all walks of life,
Airing topics cutting consciences like a knife!
*~◊~*
Over the years you shone like a beacon
With innate enthusiasm and determination!
You encouraged every woman to be a queen
Aiding them their inner beauty to be seen;
Teaching women to respect each other,
Showering them with gifts and favour!
You united relations, long lost
Bringing them together, not minding the cost!
No doubt your presence will be missed,
So three cheers to you, Ophra, I insist!
*~◊~*

## Persist in dark moments in speaking good words

Although challenging, many believers could take example from the woman of Shunem mention in Bible scripture; (2 Kings 4 verses 8-37). She refused to believe or see the negative in the <u>dark moments</u> in her life; her hope urged her towards a positive outcome and affirmed, "It is well"! (Verse 23); "It is well" (verse 26). She refused to be a hysterical woman – screaming and blaming someone else or the circumstances of the day that may have caused her son's illness and death, but pushed towards positive results. Her attitude took on faith's perspective when she declared, "it is well" while she sought it; she refused to accept that her son was dead. She believed and received the results that she craved for – her son coming back to life!

**In trusting Almighty God, it's always safe to declare –"It is well"!**

## CHAPTER 11

## YOU COULD TURN NEGATIVITY AROUND TO GOOD

Everyone has the prerogative to use their tongue to speak ill or good! The Holy Scriptures remind us that, **'Death and life are in the power of the tongue and those who love it will eat its fruit;** *(Proverbs 18v21).*

Notably, Jesus, 'the Authority on the Truth and the Life' brought this truth into perspective in his teachings when he said:

*'A good man out of the good treasure of his heart brings forth good things and an evil man out of the evil treasure brings forth evil things'.* (Mathew 12v 35)

### Adversity does not prevent good from triumphing

Adversity does not prevent good triumphing over bad: countless people blame circumstances, culture or governments for their EVERY plight in life (some of these could be proven true, but hey; – you could turn it around). There are times, however hard you may try, someone seems to move the goal post – don't throw in the towel; so to speak!

Nevertheless, adversity should not stop goodness from being expressed or demonstrated! If we study the lives of some people who had experienced dire adversity; for example, Nelson Mandela, Martin Luther King, biblical characters, Joseph and David; <u>they all left good encouraging words - telling their world that bad could be turned around to **good**</u> and that **good is preferable to bad!** These refused to become bitter victims of pessimism; rather they promoted good that benefited others and changed the course of history.

At times all types of systems and obstacles are stacked up against us as we walk life's path but if we are determined (by the grace of God) to be a 'victor' rather than being a 'victim' it could help to embolden us - spirit, soul and body if we **try to see the good** in every situation, challenge or obstacle; something I try to do every day. I'm forever seeking how I could **turn around** any and every dire situation that comes in my path for the good.

Try this example - spell these words backwards:

## STRESSED = DESSERTS

You may not like desserts, but this is to encourage you to turn adversity and other dire life's situations around to your benefit and that of others - **<u>turning adversity into a blessing</u>**!

Someone has said - FAILURE is *SUCCESS* turned inside out!

## **<u>I overcame negative encumbrance</u>**

When I was growing up many negative words were thrown in my path from all sorts of people including some relatives and school teachers; nervousness and stuttering did not help my situation either, since I became a target for their teasing.

However, since growing up, I defied negativity and prove that I have potential and that greatness is in me; furthermore that Father God has a purpose for my life. By His Favour and with determination, I am now a positive person in my outlook on life; I do not entertain any negative words spoken or written against me or anyone else. I make an assertive endeavour to turn negativity around to a positive outcome; friends have often remarked that I'm always looking for the good in people – true; **I hate negativity with a vengeance!!!**

The Poem below is one that I wrote of my experience while growing up when, my class teacher use negative words to make fun of me before my peers during an English Literature class:

**Poetic Deliverance**
~*❖*~

She was a girl who could hardly speak;
Stuttering, she would stamp her feet!
Often no words from her mouth came out
However much she wanted to shout!
~*❖*~
At School she hated registration
As to speak caused her much frustration;
So her friends answered her name in turn
To save her from flogging that would burn!
~*❖*~
To recite a Wordsworth's Poem was her task
When her Teacher made fun of her in class;
As she stuttered, some poked fun

And would at times her company shun!
~*❖*~

Tears and sadness filled her days
Compelling her to offer up prayers
To be free from speech disability
And a balm from constant misery!
~*❖*~

Like a miracle the answer finally came -
As an adult; freeing her in Jesus' name,
Through sweet 'poetic essence'
That symbolizes her deliverance!
~*❖*~

God changed trials to blessing on her behalf
And has given her the last laugh -
Showing that adversity propelled her Purpose
'For His Glory', so others could join her chorus!
~*❖*~

It is a shameful fact that there are numerous influential people, pass and present too, who endured negative banter from parents, teachers and acquaintances. Many have resisted this unconstructive pronouncement and have later triumph to become 'a magnet for change' for others and some have changed the course of history.

!!! You too could defy futile stigma and come out on a brighter and positive path of life to a lasting existence!

**People who succeeded in the face of negativity -**

(All the following, I've heard they said how they had negative statements spoken against them):

**Sporting personality Gary Lineker:** when at school a teacher spoke against his sporting abilities to become a footballer. However, he went on to become one of England's best and famed footballers and a person of influence.

**The Fastest man in the world, Usain Bolt:** his teacher had discouraged him from being an athlete; yet he is known to date as the fastest man in the world and winner of many gold medals.

**Minister, Motivational Speaker, Best Selling Author and Business-man, the late Myles Munroe,** had negative words spoken over his life by his class teacher while at school. Because he knew what great gifts were on the inside of him, he defeated it all, proving the teacher wrong and is now one of the most sought after

Motivational Speakers this century.

**Jamie Oliver, Chef and Entrepreneur**, endured negative words while at school, yet defying this he proved to the world and those who use ill words against him that he had always had great potential. He is now an influential businessman and celebrated Chef who greatly benefits his world.

There are countless others who could be added to this list and perhaps, some you may know of others, or negative encumbrance may have even happened to you!

This all points to the fact that adults have a responsibility to those they minister to. They should endeavour to look for potential talents and encourage them; even speaking good words over the lives of those whose talents are yet not visible.

When learned and influential people use their authority in ignorance to put down weak or less-able people than themselves, it is a pitiful shame!

Accordingly, the profound word of God clearly states: **'But God has chosen the foolish things of the world to put to shame the wise, and God has chosen the**

***weak things of the world to put to shame the things which are mighty; and the base things of the world and the things which are despised God has chosen...***
(See 1Corinthians 1 v 27-30).

## NO NEED FOR JEALOUSY - USE YOUR GIFTS AND TALENTS

Everyone has a gift or many gifts! Not everyone can sing like Whitney Houston or use oration excellence like Martin Luther King! Neither can everyone preach like Apostle Paul! There's no need for jealousy since, Jesus, in his teachings, told his disciples that those who believe in him should do GREATER WORKS than what he do (See St. John 14v12); Yet, Jesus was not and will never be jealous of anyone for the gifts and talents given by God our Father. Talents and Gifts are for the purpose of benefitting others!

Furthermore, Jesus is never jealous of people because Almighty God (our Father and his Father) has made us joint Heirs with him (Jesus) – after all, think what we were like before He cleanses us from sin! We should happily reject the jealousy of <u>the evil one</u> and embrace the words of Jesus in St. John 13 v34-35: ***A new commandment I give to you, that you love one another; as I have loved you that you also love one another. By this all will know that you are My disciples, if you have love for one another.***

**Think Truth! Think Right!** Suppose someone we knew who was suffering a blood disease for 38 years and eventually they were completely healed when they went up for prayer by Benny Hinn; would we be jealous that were not the one who prayed for them? - Everyone gets their gifts/talents according to God's measure! After all, the earth is full of His knowledge!

Please brothers and sisters, let us loose each other and ourselves from the entanglement of jealousy by celebrating God-given talents for Christ sake! We can't beat up God; He's the one who gave the gifts according to the Gracious Favour that is given to us - <u>He knows what each person can cope with</u>, **He gave gifts according to each person's ability**; their willingness, commitment; faithfulness; determination and what measure of effectiveness their gift would yield. (See Romans 12 v 6).

There is a diversity of gifts in the Kingdom of God. He allows every message –in whatever form - to relate to individuals appropriately, each one receive it at different levels and according to their capacity to receive. Sometimes we suppress the people we love by jealousy and resentment! <u>Gifts and talents are better effective in an atmosphere of appreciation</u>!

There are a variety of gifts which are not specified in the Bible that are a blessing, e.g. Drama; yet, there is still a need for people to appreciate some diverse gifts which are not as common as others!

We need to see through the Devil's lies – he hates believers; he is jealous of us. When believers are operating in the full and effective operation of the Gifts that Father God gave, everyone will benefit. Spiritually, we are many members in one body, i.e. (Christ) - (See Romans 12 v 4, 5). We're members one of another, so we hurt ourselves when we exercise carnal vices of jealousy and envy towards one another.

## THE LIVING WORD
~*❖*~

The **Living Word** is infallible,

For every circumstance it is suitable;

Everyone could benefit from **Word** Scripture

For free refreshment and nurture;

Mankind are favoured with access rights

To savour the **Living Word** delights!

We can never get enough of this soul food

Or discover its depth and magnitude,

But what we've read and learn we accept

And endeavour not to forget!

~*❖*~

The **Living Word** is fresh and ever current,

Always timely and inerrant!

You may say **Word** is suitably versatile,

His effect covers inch and mile!

Word is perfect for navigation,

For the Physician it is the healing medication!

Word warns sinners of Hell and destruction,

Exposing sin and points the way to Salvation!

Word is our Manual and the traveller's map,

Believe it for protection if under attack!

**Word** is good for reproof and correction,

Profitable for righteous instruction!

See Word's activity from the given theme,

That depicts a '**Word** Tree' supreme –

The **Living Word**-power a seed Creates

And fallen on good ground germinates,

Creating an entrance for the light,

Transforms blindness into sight!

Nurtured by the Spirit, **Word** motivates -

The soil of the heart generates;

Bringing changes, renewing the mind

And encourages growth sublime;

Empowering the Spirit with the Anointing that heals

And delivers the soul to fruitful yields!

~*❖*~

The Living **Word** features in the 'Beginning',

In the 'End' He sits on a horse, says Rev. 19 v 13;

However we regard Him - first, second or third,

Christ Jesus is **THE LIVING WORD**!

~*❖*~

**~**

# CHAPTER 12

## CONCLUSION

I've observed that many people in our world would seem to prefer profane words as opposed to the good ones and would readily uphold the same as their practice; causing the Lord God to give <u>warning</u> in Scripture; ***Woe to those who call evil good and good evil; who put darkness for light, and light for darkness; who put bitter for sweet and sweet for bitter!*** (Isaiah 5v20)

Despite what some people say, that only the poor, weak and insignificant people follow the Christian Faith or worship God; David, a King and Ruler over thousands of people, realise that without a relationship with the TRUE AND LIVING GOD, his life would be without meaning. The King experienced 'the power of God's Word' in his life, **using it as a bench mark by which to live** so that good success would flow in both his personal, spiritual and royal life; so much so that God affirms that King David was a man after God's heart. (See Acts 13 v 22).

Here are some declarations from his popular and universal book of Psalms concerning his experience with

God's Word:

*My tongue shall speak of Your word, for all your commandments are righteous.* (Psalms 119v172).

*Direct my steps by Your word and let no iniquity have dominion over me.* (Psalms 119v133).

*Your word is very pure; therefore Your servant loves it.* (Psalms 119v140).

## PROFOUND LASTING GOOD WORDS

No one could deny that the Christmas season brings an air of excitement to most people. The majority love Christmas (I think?); a time when people seem to get a buzz from planning and going to parties, family get-togethers, shopping for presents and expecting presents etc., etc.

At Christmas time some convey **good greetings** and send or give cards to people whom they would not normally speak to or even regard. (There is something special about Christmas – people just can't help themselves from being jolly)! Not everyone consider that Christmas stems from the fact that the celebration is because Jesus Christ was born in Bethlehem. Almighty God gave to all people, Jesus Christ as the 'Saviour' of the world, over two thousand years ago (to save them from their sin).

It is recorded in St. Luke Chapter 2 verses 10-14; that when Jesus Christ was born, God sent his Angel with these lasting GOOD WORDS to let some shepherds know about the birth: …"Do not be afraid, for behold, I bring you good tidings of great joy which will be to all people. For there is born to you this day in the City of David a Saviour, who is Christ the Lord. And this will be the sign to you: You will find a Babe wrapped in swaddling cloths, lying in a manger". And suddenly there was with the Angel a multitude of the heavenly host praising God and saying, "Glory to God in the highest and on earth peace, goodwill toward men!". **<u>Just consider the impact of those good words</u>**!

Everyone have seen and felt the effect of **the goodwill and cheer** that the Christmas season brings each year; how families and relatives come together to spend more time with each other than they would do normally.

However, we see how, each year, commercial entities have dominated the markets with their goods and services – Turkeys, various meats; Christmas cakes, mull wine; chocolates, Christmas cards; Santa's suits and hats  etc. etc. etc.; all of this proves that this **awesome message of good words** from God have such a profoundly lasting effect on people, especially children, that they cannot help themselves from being excited every time that the Christmas season comes around – why?  - Almighty God, who cannot lie, **has <u>already</u> spoken <u>GOODWILL</u> TO ALL PEOPLE!**

◊ Good Words are – beautiful, sweet, irresistible, influential, pleasant, healthy, inspiring, uplifting and encouraging; etc.

◊ Bad Words are – ugly, hurtful, degrading, evil, dark, shameful, unbecoming, damaging, humiliating; etc.

**! Good or bad words, once spoken, can never be retrieved!**

# THE (A-Z) 'WORD'

### (What essence could be found in Bible Scripture)

~ ❖ ~

| | | |
|---|---|---|
| A | - | **ASSURANCE in** His promises; |
| B | - | **BLESSINGS from** His storehouses! |
| C | - | **COMFORT for** those who mourn; |
| D | - | **DELIVERANCE from** bondages torn! |
| E | - | **EDIFICATION** for the Master's service; |
| F | - | **FAITH to** trust Him without risks! |
| G | - | **GUIDANCE for** your daily path; |
| H | - | **HEALTH that's** fully within your grasp! |
| I | - | **INSPIRATION for** every idea; |
| J | - | **JUSTICE when** found in trial's way! |
| K | - | **KINDNESS that** only God can give; |
| L | - | **LOVE ETERNAL,** so forever you may live! |
| M | - | **MERCY and** forgiveness provides; |
| N | - | **NOURISHMENT for** unhealthy lives! |
| O | - | **OPTIMISM for** future feats; |
| P | - | **PEACE for** troubled heartbeats! |

| | | |
|---|---|---|
| Q | - | **QUENCHING for** a thirsty soul; |
| R | - | **RENEWAL for** hope, spiritually cold! |
| S | - | **SATISFACTION in** times of dire scarceness; |
| T | - | **TEACHINGS in** Truth and Righteousness! |
| U | - | **UPLIFTMENT for** a stressful mind; |
| V | - | **VICTORY for** battles of every kind! |
| W | - | **WISDOM** for every difficult analysis; |
| X | - | **XENIUM as** a meaningful gift! |
| Y | - | **YIELDS of** Spiritual Fruits; |
| Z | - | **ZEST for** thriving faith-filled shoots! |

In the Revelation of Jesus Christ (See Revelation 21v27); in talking about the new Heaven and the new Earth Jesus says, ...**But there shall by no means enter it anything that defiles, or causes an abomination or a lie, but only those who are written in the Lamb's Book of Life.**

## A Rapturous Moment
~*+*~

The moment of bliss I look forward to
Is when Jesus returns for me and you?
Oh, what rapturous sights we'll behold
When our Saviour gathers us into his fold?
He has conquered that doleful enemy
To give us life with Him eternally!
That day some may be crying and weeping
For others there'll be delightful rejoicing!
Everyone could have a rapturous moment
As Father God, His son he sent
To show all people the way to live
And this 'rapturous moment' them give!

~*+*~

**~**

Accordingly, I conclude my case with some words from the Book of Psalms 50 verses (1-21) where, *Almighty God speaks to all people*. We see <u>what He *approves* and what He reproves</u>:

**The Mighty One, God the LORD, has spoken and called the earth from the rising of the sun to its going down...."Offer to God thanksgiving, and pay your vows to the Most High. Call upon Me in the day**

*of trouble; I will deliver you, and you shall glorify Me." But to the wicked God says: "What right have you to declare My statutes, or take My covenant in your mouth, seeing you hate instructions and cast My words behind you? When you saw a thief, you consented with him, and have been a partaker with adulterers. You give your mouth to evil, and your tongue frames deceit. You sit and speak against your brother; You slander your own mother's son. These things you have done, and I kept silent; You thought that I was altogether like you; But I will rebuke you, and set them in order before your eyes."*

### GIVE THANKS!
**\*\*+\*\***

In everything give thanks;

This is what God highly ranks

As a grateful attitude -

The ingredient of joy's food!

Should you be truly wise?

### You'll discern its 'Blessing' in disguise!

**\*\*+\*\***

I am confident that countless people would concur with *my 'case for good words'*; yet, predominantly, I conclude and resolve that I have the vote and endorsement of 'the God of the Universe', who is 'the leading source of **GOOD WORDS**'!

www.ingramcontent.com/pod-product-compliance
Lightning Source LLC
Chambersburg PA
CBHW070614010526
44118CB00012B/1507